THE
PLUM BEACH
LIGHT

The Birth, Life, and Death of a Lighthouse

by

LAWRENCE H. BRADNER

ACKNOWLEDGMENTS

The excerpts from *The Great Bridge*, copyright © 1972 by David McCullough, is reprinted by permission of Simon & Schuster, Inc.

Front cover from German-made post card from around 1900, courtesy of Phyllis Williams.

ISBN 0-9624248-0-3

In
happy memory of
Babbie and John,
neighbors, keepers, survivors, friends

and

In the tradition of
Leicester,
my father,
who loved The Bay,
and the art and craft of history telling

TABLE OF CONTENTS

INTRODUCTION

This book came about because some people who knew the Plum Beach Lighthouse during many of the forty-four years it was lit wanted to share with people who came later what the Light meant to us personally and what it means in a wider historical perspective.

The Light was shut off permanently in 1941 having been supplanted by the Jamestown Bridge, which had opened the previous summer; and it is hard for people who have come to Narragansett Bay since that date to appreciate the important part the Light played in guiding ships up and down the West Passage of Narragansett Bay and in keeping them off of the Plum Beach Shoal. It is also hard for newcomers to Plum Beach and the surrounding areas, when they see the dilapidated remains of the old Light, to imagine the strong feelings oldtimers have about memories of the Light as it used to be.

In the pages that follow you will find stories passed on through several generations of families, long forgotten newspaper reports, and never published documents dealing with the politics, bureaucracy, and engineering technology of instigating, building and keeping a lighthouse.

But why a full length book about a lighthouse that has been closed longer than it was operating and whose name is hardly known beyond the local area and even within the area? The simplest answer is that for a local historian places and structures may be thought of like human beings: each one has a story worth telling if only someone takes the interest and the time to pay attention to that story, and it is said that everyone, no matter what the person's life has looked like, deserves a decent burial!

But there is something more that made this book turn out the way it did. When I had nearly strained the limits of getting ideas and information from neighbors who had known the Plum Beach Light and its story more intimately than I, and after reading microfilms of the weekly editions of the Wickford *Standard* of 1897, I was left with several questions: Why was the Light built *when* it was? How was the *decision* made? What was the *method of construction?* Why did it *take so long?*

The expanded inquiry took me to the Lighthouse History Project of the State Department of Environmental Management, to the major libraries of Rhode Island, to the archives and library at the

State House, and as far away as the Coast Guard Academy Library in New London, Connecticut, the National Archives in Washington, and the office of the Coast Guard Historian in Washington. By mail and telephone I have been in touch with the Library of Congress and Kansas State University. I found two unpublished and one published doctoral dissertations which related to my subject. The results have been voluminous and significant.

It is now possible to see how the Plum Beach Light fits into not only the history of the West Passage, but also the maritime and political history of Rhode Island in the last two decades of the nineteenth century. Through the study of the origins of this lighthouse during the most prolific era of lighthouse construction in Rhode Island, it is possible to see at close hand the technology of contemporary engineering developments which made the building of such a structure possible, and at the same time to see in detail both the internal bureaucracy and the political dimensions of our nation's Light-House Board of that era.

In addition to such a narrative of facts and developments some important values and universal themes have shown up in the stories of the people who were involved with the Plum Beach Light. This story is more about people than it is about a structure. Where did people get the vigor to row up, down or across the bay a few times a day, to make back-breaking exertions of effort under the most adverse conditions, and risk their lives in the enterprise of protecting the lives and property of others? And in this present era of cracked and fallen bridges, and the *Challenger* explosion, we recognize the expertise and integrity of an engineer who pressured an administration, to make sure the Lighthouse was built safely.

Finally, in what has become obvious to many, this book has been a labor of love by this lifelong neighbor who has never forgotten how good the Lighthouse looked and sounded, and who still has a sense of loss about its closing. A happy reward for me has been the fellowship shared with neighbors, both lifelong friends and new ones, who were eager to help tell the story. An equally rewarding fellowship is that shared with other people working on lighthouse history and preservation. Lastly, the friendship and support of people without whom research would collapse, the librarians, archivists and other specialists who have preserved, catalogued, provided access to documents, treatises, and resources that tell you where to look next, and who often work without adequate budget, for the large tasks they perform.

I have been supported during the five year project by the encouragement and patience of my wife, Marcia Bradner, and of Ruth Bradner, Samuel Bradner, and Joseph Bradner, our children. I am profoundly grateful to The Right Reverend George N. Hunt, Bishop of the Episcopal Diocese of Rhode Island for help and encouragement in making possible the sabbatical leave from my responsibilities as Chaplain at the Rhode Island Medical Center during which I wrote this book. James N. Byers, the Reverend Edwin K. Packard, the Reverend Edwin Hallenbeck and Lorraine M. Belden provided significant assistance and guidance with computer technology.

The Reverend Joseph Woodson helped me to learn to write with clarity and conviction about other people and myself. The Reverend Duane Parker, the Reverend David Cargill, and the Reverend James Lassen-Willems helped me to claim commitment to a project that I deeply believed in.

The affirmation and encouragement of Donald Galamaga of the Rhode Island Department of Mental Health, Retardation and Hospitals as well as that of the Chaplains of the Medical Center Chaplains' Association helped to make the sabbatical a reality. Many thanks are due to the Reverend Janet Broadhead, the Reverend Charles LeClerc, the Reverend Edward Trafford, the Reverend James Verber, Rita Fredette, Robin Higbie, and William MacDougal, who shared with the Reverend Ida Johnson, the much appreciated coordinator, the responsibilities of the Episcopal Chaplaincy at the Medical Center during my absence.

For about fifty years I, like many others, have had the privilege of sharing simultaneously a business relationship and friendship with Bill and Helen Dwelly and their family and their associates. During the last four years this association has ripened into an opportunity of sharing many hours of stories and reflection on the history we and our forebears participated in. Helen and Bill have been an inexhaustible resource of patience, enthusiasm, and information.

The late John O. Ganze and his daughter, Alda Kaye, spent hours of thoughtful sharing not only about the Plum Beach Light, but also about a keeper's life. And the late Lewis Ganze, John's son, cordially facilitated our getting together at a significant opportunity during my research.

Earl Caswell shared stories of the 1918 Freeze at Whale Rock. Charles Cook, Rita Cook, Mr. and Mrs. Robert Eaton, Charles Arnold, Douglas Arnold, Florence Foskett, and Nancy Farin all took the time to share parts of the Plum Beach and West Passage traditions and history, most of it from first hand experience. Helen Wright, Jacqueline Wright, Mahlon Wright, and Waldo Wright contributed materials and information about 1938-1940. Helen Murray, Helen Reid, Richard Reid, Charles R. Bradner, Stephen Bradner and William M. Bradner, Jr. all gave encouragement and assistance. John Bradner was a constant consultant during the writing of Chapter IV.

Peter Crolius gave valuable consultation and affirmation during the early stages of the preparation of this book; as editor and designer he has been a knowledgeable and patient colleague in the process of creating something we both believe in.

Alicia Horan and Jerry Paquin have provided much appreciated computer expertise in preparing the text. Kenneth Ng understood what I intended to say and helped me say it more clearly. Thanks also to photographers Roger Chapman and Bill Colt. Robert Bradner shepherded me and the book through critical phases of production.

Anyone writing the history of Rhode Island lighthouses needs to begin with the seminal work of Richard Champlin, the first to undertake a systematic approach by basing his series of short histories on time-consuming interviews with keepers and their families, and by making use of contemporary newspaper reports from the eras he studied. His personal assistance and encouragement to me has been of great value.

One of the remarkable developments in the study of lighthouse history in Rhode Island has been the commitment of the state Department of Environmental Management to provide leadership in honoring both the history and the present day structures of Rhode Island lighthouses. This commitment was manifested in the leadership of D. E. M. staff member Sarah Gleason, who through her work with projects of the R. I. Parks Association, the Rhode Island Historical Preservation Commission, and the Department's own activities has done more than any other person in the state to make lighthouses and lighthouse history prominent in the public eye. All of my significant resources beyond Rhode Island, and some in Rhode Island, have been pointed out to me by Sarah.

I have appreciated the interest and advice of Professor William G. McLoughlin of the Brown University History Department, Professor Jerome Sternstein of Brooklyn College, Professor Stanley Lemons of the Rhode Island College History Department, Anthony S. Nicolosi, Director of the Naval War College Museum in Newport, and Dr. Patrick Malone of the Slater Mill. Armand Silva, Professor of Ocean Engineering at the University of Rhode Island has provided valuable hours of consultation about the engineering issues involved in establishing a foundation in the depths of the Plum Beach Shoal.

Kenneth Morse of the University of Rhode Island Library faculty and David Maslyn, the Archivist of the University Library's Special Collections Department, and Kevin Logan of that department have provided helpful leads and assistance. Thanks are due to the staff of the North Kingstown Free Library especially Susan Berman, Reference Librarian, who has always known just where to find unusual resources just right for the issue at hand, and who has patiently provided the 1896-97 microfilm reels of the Wickford *Standard* again and again, and to Anne Salisbury who persisted in getting hard-to-locate inter-library loan materials. The staffs of the Providence Public Library Reference Department, the Rockefeller Library of Brown University, and the Rhode Island Historical Society, especially the Graphics Department, have all been of great help.

Captain F. M. Hamilton, Group Commander of the United States Coast Guard at Woods Hole, Massachusetts, Mary Mackenzie, Reference Librarian of the U. S. Coast Guard Academy Library, in New London, Connecticut, John Fink and Morris Brodsky, the chief, at the Engineering Branch at the U. S. Coast Guard Shore Facilities Design and Construction office at Governor's Island, New York, have all been helpful in obtaining copies of the many still extant original engineers' drawings of the Plum Beach Light.

Dr. Robert L. Scheina, the United States Coast Guard Historian, has spent several hours sharing important insights about lighthouse construction technology and bureaucracy of the 1880's and 1890's.

Many of the individuals listed in the paragraphs above have provided valuable pictures and/or have given permission to quote from their published materials or manuscripts. To them I am profoundly grateful.

Theresa Matchette, William Sherman, and George Briscoe spent many hours in the midst of demanding schedules making available to me the resources of the Fiscal, Social, and Judicial Branch of the National Archives in Washington. They consulted with me by telephone and in person at the Archives. They provided copies of hundreds of pages of correspondence and other original material all on the Plum Beach Light coming from a variety of bound volumes and folders in the tiered stacks above their offices. I have received valuable assistance from Jenny Davis, Michael P. Musick, and Richard

Boylan of the Military Branch of the Archives, from Karen Yaffe of the Still Pictures Branch of the Archives, and from Jim Owens of the U. S. Archives Regional Office at Waltham, Massachusetts.

While I have gratitude for, and awe of, the great variety of documentary sources and of personal testimony in front of me, I take full responsibility for the characterization of the persons and events presented here.

I THE WEST PASSAGE of NARRAGANSETT BAY 1880-1899

An Overview of Maritime History

On A CLEAR EVENING just before sunset in the early summer of 1880, a passenger standing on the port side of the steamship *Rhode Island* as it made its way down the West Passage of the Narragansett Bay would have seen the islands: Patience, Prudence, Despair, and Hope, then further off beyond the East Passage, part of Aquidneck; further south the ship would pass Conanicut with Dutch Island to the west of it.

The passenger could have enjoyed the pale orange reflection of the setting sun on the tower of the lighthouse at the southern tip of Dutch Island, and just before entering the ocean, a fainter reflection on the tower of the Beavertail Light at the southern tip of Conanicut. At the same time the red light just coming on in the Dutch Island tower and the brilliant white light from the Beavertail would heighten the drama of one of the most beautiful voyages available to anyone.

A passenger at the rail on the starboard side of the same ship, one of several making a daily run to New York in that era, would have seen a more varied coast and more signs of human life on the west shore than would the passenger on the port side: first Warwick Neck, the opening of Greenwich Bay, and then the broad, low, Quonset Point, with the opening of Wickford Cove southwest of it and Fox Island south of it.

As the vessel continued south, the hills of Boston Neck would appear, running for about five miles parallel to the shore, reaching about two hundred feet in altitude at Barber's Heights above Plum Beach. In the gathering shadows the starboard passenger could see herds of cattle settling in for the night on the pastures that covered most of these hillsides, and in the space of a few minutes' time three low-lying points of land, Greene's Point, Plum Beach Point, and Casey's Point, reaching out from the sandy shore at the foot of these hills. With the help of binoculars he might see the unique birds and plant life inhabiting the recesses of the marshland and tidal ponds inside each of these points.

Immediately south of Casey's Point, and the historic Casey Farm above it, would be the small seaport village of Saunderstown, growing fast under the influence of the enterprising Stillman Saunders who built sloops and schooners and later built and operated bay steamers and steam ferryboats. Our passenger passing by on the *Rhode Island* might have seen tied up to the dock one or more of the coal-carrying schooners based in Saunderstown.

Just a mile south of Saunderstown, after passing through the narrow channel between Saunderstown and Dutch Island, our steamer would pass South Ferry. If our New York passenger on the starboard side of the *Rhode Island* had not by this time been driven inside by the chilly winds coming off the ocean just a few miles below, he would have seen on the hilltop above South Ferry the spire of the Baptist Church, and at the foot of the abruptly sloping hill houses, businesses, and factory buildings crowded around the docks.

Our passenger might have seen Captain Joseph Lester Eaton securing his catboat, the *Elizabeth,* at one of the South Ferry docks after making his daily mail run to Jamestown and/or Newport. This thirty-three year old man had since his teens singlehandedly sailed the catboat, or his family's sloops with mail freight and passengers across the bay four times a week, year 'round. He had to contend with a current that was usually challenging and with frequent fog and storms that were very challenging. An admiring contemporary writer said of Eaton, "He has missed on an average but ten trips a year . . . no more skillful boatman in the bay."

His family had dominated business at South Ferry for several generations, sailing their sloops and schooners up and down the East Coast, sometimes to the West Indies, and sailing ferries across the bay. By 1880 the once prosperous business and village were in a serious decline, and six years later, at age thirty nine, Eaton would sell all his interests at South Ferry, and in 1895 would move to Saunderstown.

Perhaps the pilot of the *Rhode Island* on this night in 1880, if he had noticed him on the dock, would have sounded the ship's whistle to greet Eaton, a fellow bay pilot, who like many others, would race out to the mouth of the bay to reach an incoming ship before his competitors and "speak" it — that is, apply to serve as its pilot going up the bay. We will sound the whistle in honor of Captain Eaton several times in this book: not only was he one of the prominent figures in West Passage maritime history but would later serve as the first Keeper of the Plum Beach Light. Now on this evening in South Ferry he might well have turned his attention to hanging out the light that burned nightly on the tall mast erected outside his house for the benefit of mariners .

Soon after South Ferry, the northeast side of that large rocky promontory, the Bonnet, would cast forbidding shadows on the steamer's wake which, in time, would roll onto the rocks at the Bonnet's base.

Within a few minutes the steamer would have left behind both Beavertail Light to the east and Whale Rock to the west. Standing as it does in deep water several hundred yards east of the south end of Boston Neck, Whale Rock serves with Beavertail as final Narragansett Bay gate markers before entering the open sea. In the gathered dusk our starboard rail passenger, heading for the cabin of the *Rhode Island*, would see the flashing white beam of the Point Judith Light five miles to the southwest.

Later in the chapter we will take a trip back up the bay through the eyes of captains and pilots. But now we turn for a further look at some enterprises of Stillman Saunders and the career of Captain Eaton. From our position in the late Twentieth Century when the West Passage is a veritable backwater, commercially speaking, these two men help us understand the extent and atmosphere of intrastate maritime activity in the West Passage and the nature of the transitions going on at that time.

Thomas Willett Stillman Saunders' family had built sloops and schooners on the Pettaquamscutt River, western boundary of Boston Neck, for several generations and since the 1850's in Saunderstown which bears their name. Because of his innovative business ventures and his involvement in many aspects of village life, Stillman made a real impact on the development of the village and on shipping in the West Passage. The move from the shallow river to Saunderstown had made possible the building of larger ships, and Stillman turned from sail to steam.

Among many ships that Saunders built and operated were the bay steamers, *Anawon* and *Wyona*. With a variety of schedules and routes in different years, these two ships ran between Providence,

Wickford, Saunderstown, and sometimes Narragansett Pier during the summers of the early nineties. Until the opening of the Sea View Rail Road in 1899 there was no satisfactory land transportation to these points. However, by the turn of the century a person who took into account where different rail routes intersected, where different ferries and steamers, operated by many different companies met each other at the same port, and where rails came near docks, could plan summer day trips up, down, across and around the bay as easily as a person in the 1980's could by transferring from bus to bus.

Edward Field cites statistics of summer travel in the bay for the year 1900 in his history of the state, *At the Turn of the Century:* the number of excursion passengers from Providence to Narragansett Pier were 33,536 on regular steamers and 19,200 on chartered; for Block Island the figures were 43,672 and 2,800.

Saunders, by a number of creative and sometimes sly moves caused all the ferry business on the west shore to be centered in Saunderstown. In the first decade of the twentieth century he operated steam ferries he had built himself between Saunderstown and Jamestown, and between Jamestown and Newport in competition with the Newport and Jamestown Ferry Company. The scope and intricate details of Saunders' activities are well laid out in Irving Sheldon's *Saunderstown* and in Anna and Charles Chapin's *Rhode Island Ferries.*

It was apparently under the influence, direct or indirect, of Stillman Saunders that Captain J. Lester Eaton moved from South Ferry to Saunderstown in 1895. While Eaton may have lacked the means and spirit to conceive and engage in such entrepreneurial ventures and innovations as his own forebears in South Ferry had done, and as Saunders was now doing, he showed a remarkable ability to face the changing times, and to take hands-on jobs that met real needs throughout his life.

Over the years Eaton's association with the ferries at Saunderstown included serving as dockmaster, quartermaster, and later as owner of a dockside fish store which he and his son Joe supplied from early morning expeditions in the catboat. He continued to serve as a bay pilot for many decades and was appointed to serve as one of the three pilot commisioners for several terms.

In 1897 the captain got involved in two entirely new activities, both indications of the Federal government's growing commitment to the safety of freight and people traveling the West Passage. The

Wickford *Standard* of May 28, 1897 tells the story in one of its typically terse items:

SAUNDERSTOWN

The United States has recently established a weather signal station in this village with Joseph L. Eaton as manager. He also has charge of the temporary light and fog signal at the proposed Plum Beach Lighthouse.

The October 1, 1987 issue of that weekly newspaper adds that the pole of the weather station is "65 feet in height on an elevation 85 feet above sea level," and that the signals are visible "from Wickford Flats to Beavertail."

Regarding Eaton's lighthouse assignment, Richard Champlin, in his comprehensive history of Rhode Island Lighthouses in the Spring, 1971 Bulletin of the Newport Historical Society, writes that the Captain "rowed up from Saunderstown every evening, or else sailed his catboat, the *Elizabeth,* to hang a temporary lantern on the caisson (of the half-finished structure)." That would have meant rowing a mile and a half each way, often against a stiff current and occasionally against vigorous northeasters and winter storms.

Perhaps this tall, muscular individual was hired not only for his reputation for strength and physical endurance but also for his reputation for unfailing response to any commitment he made. Joseph Lester Eaton was a staunch son of the state in which water had been the chief means of transportation for two centuries after its founding as a colony by Roger Williams (who at age seventy-three rowed all day and half the night from Providence to Newport for a theological discussion).

If we are to understand fully the commercial importance of Narragansett Bay, its West Passage and its lighthouses in particular, we must look at the whole state and see how the burgeoning Rhode Island manufacturing economy during the second half of the last century and the availability of increasingly larger steam vessels brought about a resurgence in the volume of shipping going up and down the Atlantic seaboard. (However, the decline in the bay's foreign trade which occured in the first few decades of the nineteenth century was never significantly reversed.)

Manufacturing interests located throughout the state, and extensively in northern Rhode Island, needed raw materials shipped in and their products shipped out. These raw materials included lumber and the cotton which was so important for the textile mills, but statistics from the last few years of the century show that the most prominent incoming cargo was coal, which by that time was indispensable for industry and important for heating many private homes. Sometimes one tug pulled a whole string of barges loaded with coal up the bay.

In addition to New York and Philadelphia there was shipping to the Central States; for example, the Merchants and Miners' Transportation Company of Boston established the Providence, Norfolk, and Baltimore Line in 1873. In the late 90's this line operated up to four passenger and freight vessels running twice a week, and in some years three times a week between those cities and Newport News. In 1898 the *Providence Journal of Commerce* described two of their ships as follows, "... magnificent ... first class passenger accommodations ... of 3,000 tons register ... carrying capacity of 160 carloads of freight."

We get a comprehensive picture of the maritime traffic in the Rhode Island area during the busy years of this nineteenth century shipping revival from the Wickford *Standard's* December 7, 1894 report on the number of ships passing Point Judith in 1893:

Steamers	12,000
Schooners	34,000
Sloops	2,000
Yachts	7,000
Ships	200
Barges	9,600
Brigs and Brigantines	200
Total Tonnage	30,260,000

A consistent theme in the literature of, and about, this period is the increase in draught-depth, width and capacity of both the steamers and sailing vessels. In fact, the demise of the Eatons' once prosperous business was a result of the inability of their fleet of 75-to 300-ton vessels to compete with the larger ships being built in the 1870's.

Field's *At the Turn of the Century* gives both opinion and statistics: "... After the War of Rebellion...the size of coastwise vessels has materially increased ... Especially true of coal carrying vessels, which formerly brought cargoes of 200 or 300 tons, while the present barges and schooners engaged in that trade carry from 600 to 2,500 tons or more." This theme had significant bearing on the decision of the U.S. Government to build the Plum Beach Light and to make many other improvements in the bay during this era.

Now that we have seen the great need for shipping in Narragansett Bay and something of the type and size of vessels in that period, the appearance of new lighthouses can be better explained if we know who operated the ships.

An overview of the dozens of coastwise steamship companies taking freight and passengers in and out of the bay during the last third of the nineteenth century shows a picture of constant fluctuation: fires, shipwrecks, lucrative successes, financial disasters, and mergers. Of significance was the linking up of rail and steamer service at New London, Norwich, Stonington, Fall River, and most importantly for our study, at Providence.

The overall trend was away from ownership by Rhode Islanders and others who built and operated their own ships or who owned manufacturing companies that shipped goods on their own lines to ownership by large regional conglomerates with the railroads and Wall St. barons taking over control. By 1895 the New York, New Haven, and Hartford Railroad had gained control of almost all Long Island Sound steamers and all railroads between the ports mentioned above and New York and Boston.

One of the most enduring companies, and for our study the most significant, was the Providence and Stonington Steamship Company, formed in 1875 after its first president, Capt. D. S. Babcock, had been simultaneously elected president of the Providence and New York Steamship Company and of the Stonington Steamship Company. He was already vice president of the Stonington Railroad which had formed Stonington Steamship!

A later president of the Providence and Stonington, J. W. Miller, who became instrumental in pushing the decision to build the Plum Beach Light, showed how important the West Passage was to the P. and S. in his July 14, 1892 letter to the Light House Board:

> The tonnage passing up and down the Western Passage is exceedingly large and the value of our freight alone per annum amounts to $100,000,000, and the passengers during the five months we run passenger boats during the summer is about 50,000.

That picture presents such a contrast to the inactivity of the West Passage and the low level of shipping in the still dredged channels of the East Passage in the late twentieth century, that it is useful to see the explanation of the patterns of bay shipping explained in *The Providence Daily Journal* of May 10, 1896:

> The east or middle passage has 25 feet of water, but it is a less direct route to Providence, and in thick weather vessels to and from this city are liable to collide with those trading at Newport and Fall River. The value of the west passage to Providence is obvious.

Having now made this general survey of the shipping on the bay near the end of the last century and a more detailed and personalized study of local shipping in the West Passage, it is now time to see what new aids to navigation and improvements to channels and harbors were needed for this shipping and to see who did something about those needs. That means taking the return voyage up the bay promised to the readers following that hypothetical early summer 1880 trip down the bay on the steamer *Rhode Island* at the beginning of the chapter — but this time through the eyes of captain and pilot.

It would not be advisable to plan our return trip on the run of the *Rhode Island* which departed from the dock in New York shortly after 5 o'clock Friday night, November 5, 1880 with about one hundred passengers on board and about $75,000 worth of freight, including cotton for Providence and hemp and leather for Boston. This ship, referred to as a "palace steamer" built by Capt. William P. Williams for the old Stonington Line in 1873 and inherited by the P. and S., began its last run on that foggy Friday night.

After passing uneventfully through the first part of the night in very thick fog, after passing around Point Judith successfully, and after picking up the signal of Beavertail, the *Rhode Island* ended the run and its career with a tumultuous crash onto the rocks about 75 feet from shore near the north side of the Bonnet between 3:00 and 3:30 on the morning of November 6th. Fortunately no one was killed, although some were injured, and many drenched. Some equipment, freight, and luggage were saved, but the ship was a total loss. Captain Joseph Eaton directed a fleet of boats which removed cotton and other freight to nearby schooners. One hundred years later his family

The wreck of the *Rhode Island* at The Bonnet, 6 November, 1880.

Courtesy of Peabody Museum of Salem.

still has a Bible donated to the ship by the New York Bible Society salvaged by the captain along with the paying freight.

If we were to plan our return trip up the bay for the 1882 season on the new *Rhode Island*, which the Providence and Stonington put in service that year to replace the wrecked ship, we might see the new lighthouse on Whale Rock under construction. It was U. S. Representative from Rhode Island, Nelson W. Aldrich, who wrote to the U. S. Light-House Board the day after the demise of the old *Rhode Island* about the need for a light on Whale Rock (which had been discussed in Congress since 1876). A Providence *Journal* editorial writer of November 10, 1880, blamed the loss of the old *Rhode Island* a few days before on the lack of a lighthouse on that rock.

However we might wish to delay our return trip up the bay several years until more aids to navigation had been provided to safeguard our journey. We would certainly want to avoid signing on to the P. and S. steamer *Pequot* any time during the winter-spring of 1891-2. During that time the hardy ship endured a collision, a grounding and sinking, a fire, and another grounding — this one on Casey's Point.

If we choose the spring of 1896 for our voyage to Providence we would find merchants, political leaders, shipowners and captains with a more optimistic outlook on the future of Narragansett Bay shipping than at any other time during the period of this study.

We will sign on the *Governor Ames*, a five masted schooner with Capt. C. A. Davis, commander and managing owner. Considered the largest schooner in the world, at that time, with a capacity for 3,000 tons of coal, the *Governor Ames*, during the spring of 1896, was on annual lease to a Providence coal company.

Our signing on a coal schooner in early April, 1896 would leave us with some uncertainty about date and time of arrival. Ordinarily it took from two to four days to sail from Norfolk, but schooners coming from that city, Newport News, and Philadelphia experienced delays causing one to take nine days due to "remarkably small amount of wind," as the April 17 *Journal* reports.

On our hypothetical journey with the *Governor Ames*, the captain and the pilot we would pick up after coming around Point Judith would be even more interested than our two 1880 Providence-to-New York passengers in seeing the islands and points of the West Passage but not because of their beauty. They would want to *avoid* the islands and points, and the shoals which stretched out under the water near some of them.

In the early evening of this April day, catching sight of the fixed red light shining from the Whale Rock Lighthouse and the white flashes of the Beavertail a mile-plus to the east would help the schooner make a good entrance into the West Passage. The Whale Rock Light not only would protect against hitting the rock itself and beaching on the Bonnet, it also would help in setting the course up the bay. Traveling the West Passage by day could be challenging, but traveling at night, during fogs, and storms, or a combination of these, put ships in critical danger. This was long before the invention of radar, but lighthouses, buoys, bell buoys, and gas-lighted buoys made it possible to face the challenge.

The Dutch Island Light, burning since 1857, would help the schooner avoid the island itself; but, in the gathering darkness with moderate fog now rolling in, this lighthouse wouldn't keep us from *overdoing* avoiding the island and ending up on Casey's Point on the west shore or, further north, running into the Plum Beach Shoal which extends from Plum Beach Point in an easterly direction halfway across the Passage. Instead of facing such a risk, Captain Davis might have decided and, for our story here, did to come around the north side of Dutch Island and spend the night in Dutch Island Harbor, where a ship at anchor would not be such a target for steamers coming through the fog. A departure shortly before dawn would enable the *Ames* to reach difficult spots in the northern part of the West Passage and in the Providence River before the tide would start to go out around 10:30 A.M. The incoming tide itself would assist the southwest winds in bringing the schooner up the bay to meet the tug.

Proceeding north slowly before dawn the next morning with the fog still hanging in the lower part of the bay, the pilot on the *Governor Ames* would catch sight of the lighted gas buoy, moved a short distance during the past month to the south-east edge of Plum Beach Shoal (about half a mile south of the future lighthouse). Prior to February 19, 1896 the only protection against the shoal was a bell buoy.

Continuing north, with the fog beginning to lift, the pilot might see the fixed red light from the lighthouse built on Conanicut Point at the north end of that island in 1886; and further east, beyond the lighthouse he would see a pink-orange glow coming into the sky over Aquidneck Island.

With visibility improved by the rising sun and the disappearance of the fog, the next challenge for the *Governor Ames*, would be passage over a section halfway between Allen's Harbor and the northern end of Prudence Island, where the narrow channel's depth at mean low water is less than 24 feet; (a similar section about half a mile long comes later to the east of Rocky Point). Fortunately Captain Davis's early start from Dutch Island Harbor would enable us to cross these points before heavy traffic and low tide might make it awkward.

Coming north on the main channel into the Providence River the Captain would call for the remaining sails to be brought down at the sight of a tug steaming down from Nayatt Point with whistle blowing. The tug would have been alerted by a telephone call from Captain Eaton in Saunderstown who communicated regularly with the Providence Tow Boat Co. to tell them of incoming ships.

By the time the *Governor Ames*, pulled by the tug, would have proceeded slowly up the winding narrow channel from Conimicut Point Light to the southeast side of Field's Point, it would be close to noon, the tide already starting to go out. There would be a lot of traffic going both ways just north and south of the sandbar which stretches east from the Point, and leaves only a narrow channel close to the rocks on the east side. The sandbar has been known to shift by as much as 28 feet in a single storm. Again, with the tide going out, it would be better to wait over the noon hour until traffic diminished and there would be more room to negotiate the narrow channel.

Following the completion of this hypothetical voyage, at the dock of the coal company we might well join the pilot in a drop-in visit to the Chairman of the Pilot Commissioners, Frank M. Burrough, at his South Water St. Office where he handled both his commercial business in oils and cotton and his Commission work.

Burrough was a merchant in the sense that the word is not generally used today: A merchant brought in raw materials and/or finished goods which he supplied to others, and was also involved in the transportation process by which the material arrived. Until railroads started coming into prominence in the mid-nineteenth century ships had been the only significant transportation into Providence. Burrough was thoroughly involved at various levels in the whole process of shipping into Providence.

Our pilot might well have come to see Commissioner Burrough to complain about the usual trouble coming around Field's Point and to thank Burrough for his successful efforts in obtaining the lighted gas buoy at Plum Beach earlier the same year. Over a period of at least twenty years Burrough was the most consistent and persistent advocate for improvements, by the federal government, in aids to navigation in the Narragansett Bay.

In the instance of the Plum Beach buoy, which he had first petitioned for as far back as 1882, Burrough had on January 1, 1896 sent to the Light-House Board a petition which represented not only the pilots, as most of his petitions did, but was also signed by the Governor, the Mayor, Captain Davis, the captains or agents of the leading steamship lines, the Board of Trade, and many others including Burrough's distant cousin, John Nicholas Brown, "owner of the steam yacht, *Ballymena.*" The Petition asked for "Pintch-lighted buoys" at "Plumb Beach" and six other locations in the bay.

In response to the complaints during this bay pilot's visit, Burrough might well have pulled out and handed to his visitor the April 18, 1896 issue of the Providence *Journal* pointing to the article headed "Channel Improvements." The article stated the confidence Providence Mayor Edwin D McGuiness and U.S. Senator from Rhode Island, Nelson W. Aldrich, had about the expected results of a proposed amendment to the 1896 River and Harbor Bill.

The amendment provided for a channel at least 25 feet deep at mean low water, at least 400 feet wide along the route followed by the *Governor Ames* in our hypothetical journey, and, in particular, called for dredging the shallow channel west of Prudence and east of Rocky Point. At Field's Point not only was dredging out the sandbar called for, but also actually cutting back the point itself about 300 feet up to the dining hall. The price-tag for the proposed appropriation: $732,820.

This 1896 project was to be the culmination of campaigning, surveys, and actual dredging which had gone on sporadically since 1853 and had gradually improved channels in the bay and the Providence River. The constituency immediately affected by these developments included Providence merchants, manufacturers, shipowners, captains, pilots, and politicians. However, the manufacturers and the merchants, Burrough excepted, seemed to have taken a back seat in campaigning for such projects. The wider constituency affected by Rivers and Harbors legislation and by the establishment of aids to navigation such as lighthouses and buoys was the entire state, whose predominant manufacturing economy required good transportation and whose passsengers still made significant use of water travel.

In the area of maritime commerce there were two closely related reasons for supporting the project; both of them come out in quotes from captains in one of at least five Providence *Journal* stories during that spring. One reason is obvious after our recent trip into Providence on the *Governor Ames*, and Captain Davis expressed it to the *Journal* :

There is a fleet of large schooners running to the port at present, vessels which carry over 2,000 tons, which need plenty of water, which will be vastly benefited by the dredging out of the channel and the cutting off of the points which at present make dangerous turns in the course. We shall all see these difficulties abolished with pleasure.

Captain Walter R. Hazard, a commander of the Providence and Stonington Steamship Company said it with stronger feeling:

The legislative action which has appropriated millions for the rivers and harbors has never before got down to hard pan on this matter. But it was sure to come, had to come. . . This plan will cut off three very plaguesome points in the bay and river. . . I would like to see a list of the hundreds of vessels which have grounded on [Field's] point or got into difficulties on account of its proximity. It has been a matter of serious difficulty to navigate big vessels through the narrow passage between the end of the bar . . . and Fuller's Rock in foggy weather. Chances are taken in thick weather of unavoidably losing hundreds of thousands in steamboat property.

Captain Davis stated the second reason for supporting the project, expressing the optimism he and the other captains felt about the future of the port of Providence:

. . .The people of Providence and of the State will have good reason to congratulate themselves. The advantages of the port as a distributing centre can be developed, as a first-class harbor with a good waterway leading to it will draw shipping. Providence has a great future before it as a maritime centre, and this is one of the longest steps which has been made in that direction.

Our voyage to Providence on the *Governor Ames* arrived soon enough for us to get a timely announcement of a speech to be given on April 25, 1896 at the Providence Commercial Club by the new Mayor of Providence, Edwin D. McGuinness, whose title was to be "The Commercial Future of Providence."

Those in attendance on April 25 got a sense of the Mayor's great optimism and a cordial poke:

The favorable geographical location of Providence as a distributing commercial centre, is apparent from a glance at the map of New England. Besides this, it is a safe harbor for entrance at all conditions of tide, and cargoes may be delivered from the vessels to the cars with the least delay and expense. The encouraging increase of late years in the water's tonnage of this port is an index of the great future that awaits us. What we need expecially, in the first instance, is a determined, intelligent, courageous public spirit among our representative business men; a spirit that will carry out all measures tending to the improvement of our foreign commerce, and especially to obtain from Congress such assistance as will give us safe navigation for deep-draught vessels in both east and west passages of the bay.

. . .I wish to here make due acknowledgement of the assistance rendered by our representatives in Congress in forwarding [the pending river and harbor bill]. But. . . "God helps those that help themselves." The deep interest taken by the representatives of the different steamboat lines connecting with our city, of the Pilot Commissioners and the members of What Cheer Association of Harbor Pilots and Masters in the improvement of navigation in Narragansett Bay, by widening and deepening the channel, and placing proper fog and light signals is an encouraging sign of the growth of a public sentiment in the community that will in the near future bring forth beneficial results.

. . .Among the possibilities of united and persistent effort, I see a passenger line the year around to New York; a direct line by water to Savannah and other southern ports; a direct fruit trade to the West Indies; and a line to Europe and Japan.

The *Providence Journal of Commerce* in reporting this speech threw in the caustic comment that it was an "almost unheard of thing for the Commercial Club. . . (an organization having on its roll of membership the names of some of the leading manufacturers and merchants of New England) to be addressed . . . upon a subject bearing upon the future greatness of Providence as a commercial city."

In the following (July, 1896) issue the same *Journal* praised Senator Aldrich and Representative Melville Bull for their efforts. The bill had been passed on June 3rd. Aldrich was a consistent supporter of Rivers and Harbors legislation. Representative Bull took pride in his efforts to pass such legislation.

On June 11th, 1896 a bill was passed appropriating $40,000 to begin and complete the construction of the Plum Beach Light for which an initial outlay of $20,000 had been voted a year before. Why the decision to build the Plum Beach Light had taken fourteen years, and why the construction took another three years will come out in the next two chapters.

II THE DECISION TO BUILD

Beached Ships and Bureaucracy

AN INITIAL LOOK at the period which begins with the first surviving reference to a lighthouse at Plum Beach in 1882 and ends with the act of Congress in 1895 which approved the project presents a confusing picture.

This chapter tries to draw out the clarity that can be genuinely found without abusing the complexity that is a real part of the story. Readers who have no stomach for speculations about political and bureaucratic ambiguities may wish to pass on to Chapter III!

Chapter I has already briefly introduced you to the Chairman of the Rhode Island Pilot Commissioners, Frank M. Burrough, to the Providence and Stonington Steamship Company, and United States Senator from Rhode Island, Nelson W. Aldrich, a name still well known to many in the late twentieth century. All of them had significant roles in the decision to build the lighthouse. We have yet to introduce the central character in the story, The United States Light-House Board.

The Light-House Board was created by Congress in 1852 as a result of an investigation which showed the previous lighthouse administration to be corrupt, badly managed both administratively and financially, and technically inadequate to meet the needs of safe and profitable maritime transportation.

The original involvement of the federal government in lighthouses had begun with an act of Congress on August 7, 1789, calling for federal funding for the aids to navigation of a nation made up almost entirely of maritime states. From the manuscript of Sarah Gleason's comprehensive forthcoming book, *Kindly Lights*, we get, in a few words, an overview of the initial stages of the federal efforts.

. . . In this first piece of public works legislation, the young government in principle guaranteed equal protection to all vessels sailing its coasts. To fund the maintenance of its navigational aids, Congress chose the French method of a general appropriation rather than the British policy of taxing passing vessels. But while this act symbolized the end of local control over facilities meant to benefit everyone, in practice it was 63 years before this ideal came to pass.

The intent of Congress 63 years later in 1852 was to gather together in one leadership body the greatest expertise they could get in the areas of maritime needs, scientific knowledge, engineering technology and economic administration. The act stated:

The President shall appoint two officers of the Navy of high rank, two officers of the Corps of Engineers of the Army, and two civilians of high scientific attainment, whose services may be at the disposal of the President, together with an officer of the Navy and an officer of the engineers of the Army, as secretaries, who shall constitute the Light-House Board. The Secretary of the Treasury shall be ex officio president of the Light-House Board.

With the help of further acts the board set up sixteen light-house districts. Rhode Island, Connecticut, the Atlantic and Hudson coastlines of New York, and part of New Jersey were included in the Third Light-House District. Each district had a naval officer as inspector and an officer of the Army Corps of Engineers as district engineer.

The new board took on a prodigious responsibility; it included professionalizing the light-house personnel at all levels, publishing an annual List providing mariners with exact locations and distinguishing characteristics of each United States lighthouse, all buoys and other aids to navigation, replacing inadequate lamps, lenses, and other equipment with vastly superior modern types of equipment already used by European nations for many years, and building new lighthouses in the many places where they were needed.

In Rhode Island alone the success of the Light-House Board's efforts are well illustrated by the twenty new lighthouses built between 1854 and the end of the century, the rebuilding of seven of the nine earlier lights, and the rebuilding of three of those more recently built by the Board itself, to say nothing of the multitude of floating aids to navigation such as buoys.

There is much to be said to the credit of the Light-House Board's accomplishments during its existence between 1852 and 1910; however, its own success dictated its ultimate demise. In *America's Lighthouses* Francis Ross Holland Jr., after describing positively some of the developments presented above, goes on to say, "As time went on, though, the nine-member Light-House Board proved to be too cumbersome an administrative head to manage effectively and efficiently the country's aids to navigation." The Board, having its regular meetings only four times a year and having the naval and engineer secretaries with their own distinct responsibilities as the only full-time personnel on the Board itself, could not adequately manage the vast national system it had done so well to create.

Consequently the reorganization of 1910, which eliminated the Light-House Board, created the national Light House Service under the direction of a single Commissioner, so that decisions that had to be made on the national level could be made more efficiently. It delegated more authority to the district Superintendents to make decisions on the spot.

In our look at the Board's role in Rhode Island lighthouse activity during the last two decades of the century we can see results of its technological advancements and the expertise, integrity and persistence on the part of some of its staff. But the history of the Plum Beach Light and others of this era was also affected by the Board's frugality and ineptitude. Moreover, the Board tended to take a *reactive* stance in two important related areas. Construction of new lighthouses and the installation of new floating aids to navigation, when construction and installation happened, originated from shipowners and politicians petitioning the Board rather than from the Board initiating and pursuing a planned program of operational development. Likewise, within the structure of government, the Board apparently lacked the political will and capacity to advocate aggressively for the financial support of its mission.

Finally, it must be said, that with partly understandable caution, the Board did not take on until the 1880's and 90's the three most challenging projects in Rhode Island: Whale Rock at the southwest edge of the entrance to the West Passage, the rocks off Sakonnet Point at the southeastern corner of the state and the Plum Beach Shoal. Of course the most famous Rhode Island lights, Beavertail and the Point Judith, are in very rough locations; however, the lighthouses themselves were built on easily accessible, dry ground. But lighthouses completely surrounded by water are referred to as *waveswept*. Of course there are waveswept locations in protected northern waters of the bay and the Providence River where lights were needed or already built. But these three, Whale Rock, Sakonnet Point, and Plum Beach, are the only waveswept locations where frequent rough weather could be expected.

The significance of the Whale Rock and Sakonnet Point locations cannot be overestimated, keeping in mind both the need to point vessels on their way into the mouth of the bay and the need to avoid the rocks on which they stand. But the challenge of building and maintaining lights there was exacerbated by the continuing onslaught of rough weather at those locations. The Plum Beach location, while somewhat more protected from ocean storms than the other two, is subject to the buildup of northeast winds coming down the bay, is about half a mile away from the mainland, and provides no rock upon which to base a foundation; the location is, simply, seventeen feet of water over a shoal of sand in the middle of the West Passage.

The two real champions in the cause of dealing with the Plum Beach Shoal were The Providence and Stonington Steamship Company and Pilot Commissioner Frank M. Burrough. Burrough and Zebediah Williams, Providence agent of the company, both wrote to Senator Aldrich in the year 1882 about Plum Beach. The first reference to a lighthouse on the Plum Beach Shoal comes in Agent Williams' letter in November of that year; and we will quote from it later while looking at other campaigning done by his company.

But the first recorded instance now available to us of a request dealing with Plum Beach comes in a July 6, 1882, letter from Burrough to Nelson W. Aldrich, who only nine months earlier had been elected by the General Assembly to fill the U.S. Senate seat of the recently deceased General Burnside. We have the letter copied in Burrough's handwriting from the Light-House Board correspondence in the National Archives:

Hon! Nelson Aldrich

Dear Sir.

　　Will you oblige me by applying your influence in such directions, as will secure a "Whistling buoy" at a point one mile S. S. W. of "Beaver Tail Light house," and a lighted buoy "off Plumb beach" West passage. Narragansett Bay.

F. M. Burrough
Capt. Sherman
" "   Willis
Pilot Comm. of RI

Copy

We learn several things about Burrough from this letter written on the stationery of his oils and cotton firm at 22 South Water St. in Providence:

Although he apparently never in his life served as a pilot, Burrough was very up-to-date and knowledgeable about the technology of aids to navigation. Within a year of the first use by the Light-House Board of lighted buoys containing compressed gas which burns inside a well-sealed lens, Burrough in this letter is requesting one for Plum Beach. Two years later in Washington, D. C., he attended the "Exhibition of the Marine Night Signals before the 'Board of Officers' appointed by the 'Bureau of Navigation' and Signal Service," tries to get Aldrich to make Congress adopt the system, and explored the possibility of helping form a company to provide it.

But the 1882 letter about Plum Beach and the nine letters from Burrough in the Library of Congress Aldrich Collection raise questions about what sort of relationship the two men had. The questions about their relationship are of interest because of the kind of response Aldrich made to Burrough's requests about Plum Beach.

Burrough addresses the Senator with a tone that varies from formal to familiar and from jaunty to provocative and pushy. He greets Aldrich with "Friend Aldrich-" in a November, 1881 letter soon after the twice elected Rhode Island member of the House of Representatives had been elevated to the Senate following the death of Burnside, and, omitting any congratulations, recommends a Capt. Hussey who is about to approach Aldrich about "your taking an interest in a vessel."

Burrough uses the greeting "Friend Nelson" in an 1889 letter and asks for the Senator's signature on a petition to the Governor to get him appointed to a state board. In the 1882 letter about the Marine Night Signals system exhibit he begins with a businesslike "Dear Sir," and, after declaring the exhibition "a decided success," continues with an emphatic take-charge demeanor: "Now then. I want the subject brought before Congress and a recommendation that the System be adopted. . . Your efforts will be appreciated. . . Awaiting your reply."

In the Night Signals letter the Pilot Commission technologist and the would-be entrepreneur are one. He is eager to push a promising deal in an innovative business.

There is reason to assume that these two Rhode Islanders were well acquainted. They were both born in 1841, were young businessmen in Providence in the early 1870's, and were members of the Squantum Association.

But there were some differences. Frank Burrough, even though he had spent some of his earlier years away from Rhode Island, came from an old Providence mercantile family — which was related to such Providence aristocrats as the Powers, the Cookes, and the Browns. Frank's great uncle, Robert S. Burrough, Sr., served in the U.S. Customs House in Providence from its inception in 1790 and for nearly forty years thereafter.

Nelson Aldrich, on the other hand, came from Foster with background in other rural parts of Rhode Island, Massachusetts and Connecticut. He was a largely self-educated and a self-made man in the best sense. After he arrived in Providence on his own as a teenager, his rise in business and later in politics was dramatically fast. Beginning with work in a fish store in 1860, a book-keeping job in a large grocery wholesale firm, leading to partnership, he was elected to the Providence Common Council from the Fifth Ward in 1869, then, through several steps, to Speaker of the House in the General Assembly by the year 1876, on to his first election to the U.S. House in 1878, and after entering the Senate in1881 remaining until 1911. His success was a credit to his singular intellectual ability and energetic motivation; but there was more to it than that.

Without censoring the raw facts and with balanced treatment of character, two Brown University authors, William G. McLoughlin, Professor of History, in his *Rhode Island, a History,* and Jerome Sternstein in his Ph. D. dissertation, *Nelson Wilmarth Aldrich,* have shown that it took more than intellect and motivation to get Aldrich as far as he went.

There were two keys to Aldrich's success. First, in his leadership of tariff legislation for twenty five years he showed a well researched, studious, and attentive concern for business profits for manufacturers in Rhode Island, New England, and the United States. Second, his political alliance with U. S. Senator Henry Anthony from Rhode Island and with a Rhode Island Republican Party machine boss, General Charles R. Brayton, kept Aldrich's local political infrastructure well articulated while the Senator retained a more lofty statesmanlike posture on a national level. His political stature and power grew to the point where he became known as the "General Manager of the United States."

We may well conjecture whether Burrough had a mixture of respect for Aldrich's power and ability on the one hand, and, coming, as Burrough did, from an old line Providence background, which by this time is a *dignified* background, some resentment about needing the help of this aggressive and politically shrewd newcomer. It would not be the only time in Providence history for such a shift in power and for such reaction to the shift. In the case of Burrough the extent of the shift was to be ironically dramatized when Aldrich in the 1890's first rented and then bought the imposing house designed for Burrough's great uncle, Robert S. Burrough, Sr., in the 1820's by John Holden Greene. The house, standing at the corner of Benevolent and Cooke streets, now called the "Aldrich House," belongs to the Rhode Island Historical Society. In the same decade that Aldrich bought the house, Frank Burrough's domicile shifted every few years to houses of considerably more modest status.

But, then, how did Aldrich feel about hearing from Burrough? And how did he feel about getting two different letters from Burrough about Plum Beach, the 1882 letter we quoted above and the letter of 1884?

"Senator Aldrich believed implicitly that the people did not know what was good for them in the way of legislation and so read with curiosity and amusement the great mass of letters always piled on his desk," says David Barry in one of the lengthy articles in the Providence *Journal* of April 17, 1915, the day after Aldrich died. Barry went on to say, "He was very lax in attending to all his correspondence and habitually used the telephone in preference to the mails and the telegraph." Sternstein confirms Barry's facts, if not the interpretation, explaining that Aldrich was averse to commiting himself in writing.

In view of the Senator's unwillingness to commit himself in writing about many issues, some of the comments about Aldrich in this chapter have to be taken as the speculations that they are, even though the comments appear to be borne out substantially in the patterns other commentators have observed.

However, actions speak louder than words. The day after receiving Burrough's 1882 letter about Plum Beach, Aldrich forwarded it to the Light-House Board with the most perfunctory covering letter stating no more than the fact that he is enclosing the Pilot Commissioners' letter and mentioning its subject matter.

Two years later on April 24, 1884 Commissioner Burrough makes a stronger and more explicit request about Plum Beach, writing to Aldrich from the Fifth Avenue Hotel at Madison Square in New York City:

Dear Sir

I have been requested, by a large number of our merchants, to write you, asking for your efforts to secure for the benefit of our Commerce in Providence, R. I. the building of a "Light House" at "Plum Beach Point," West Passage, Narragansett Bay, also a "Lighted Buoy" in place of Can Buoy No.7 off the end of the Shoal South of Conimicut Point Light. Both positions are now practically unprotected in thick weather.

Very respectfully,
F. M. Burrough
Pilot Commissioner

To
Hon: Nelson W. Aldrich
Washington, D.C.

The formality in a letter he hopes will be forwarded is obvious; it is also gratifying to note that this time he has spelled properly the subject of this story.

This time the Senator's action is an outright snub to the cause of a light at Plum Beach, but at least it makes a clear stand. His letter to the Light-House Board a few days after hearing from Burrough says,

I beg to call to your attention to the enclosed letter from F. M. Burrough, Pilot Commissioner from Rhode Island, especially in regard to what he says of the necessity for a lighted buoy in place of Can Buoy N. 7 off the end of the Shoal south of Conimicut Point Light.

Very truly yours,
Nelson W. Aldrich

Ten days after his April 24 letter to Aldrich Burrough sent him a post card, in preparation for his coming trip to Washington, requesting Aldrich to "call upon me at the Arlington Hotel on Wednesday morning next, May 7, 1884." It was apparently the same trip during which Burrough visited the Night Signals exhibition.

We shall probably never find out what Burrough learned about Aldrich's communication to the Board or about Aldrich's views on a lighthouse at Plum Beach. However, Sternstein gives us a clue to what might have transpired with a quotation he cites from Senator Stephen Benton Elkins of West Virginia who was asked by a reporter to explain the source of Aldrich's power.

Suppose there is something you want very much indeed. You go to Aldrich to get him to agree to let you have it. He talks to

R.I. Pilot Commissioner Burrough's April 1884 letter to Senator Aldrich.

From Nelson W. Aldrich papers at the Library of Congress.

you about it and after five minutes you go out. You have ceased to want the thing that you want and now you want the thing that Aldrich wants.

He goes on to refer to "the subtle, often devious, sometimes brutal, always hidden process by which Aldrich moves people to do his bidding." We can only guess what happened between these two Rhode Islanders at the Arlington on the morning of May 7, or whether Aldrich persuaded Burrough to meet him somewhere else. We can even conjecture, on the basis of Elkins' comment, whether Burrough's excitement about putting together a company to provide a system of Night Signals originated from Aldrich!

We do know that there is no further preserved or known communication between them about Plum Beach. But any disappointment he may have had about Plum Beach did not stop Burrough from writing the Senator on other subjects until at least 1889. Because of the decreasing number of all incoming letters from the 1890's preserved in the Aldrich Collection at the Library of Congress, it is hard to tell whether Burrough gave up trying to get favors from Aldrich or whether some later letters were discarded.

In the mid 1890's Burrough tried another approach to securing aids to navigation for the bay: he wrote directly to the Light-House Board with public encouragement of the Board of Trade's *Providence Journal of Commerce*, which chronicles and praises the many successful transactions with the Light-House Board by the "enterprising," "indefatigable" Pilot Commissioner between 1895 and 1898. The editor probably did not know how long Burrough had waited for two of his successes: In early 1896, more than six months after the Congress made the preliminary appropriation for the lighthouse at Plum Beach, he got the Board to place on the shoal the lighted buoy he had first requested through Aldrich in 1882 and, in 1898, the gas lighted buoy for Conimicut Point Shoal he had requested in 1884.

The *Providence Daily Journal* writer of the May 27, 1903 front page story about Burrough's death on a train in Boston the previous day failed to do justice to the complexity of the man's character. While a few of his accomplishments are fairly accurately, if briefly, presented, Burrough comes across as a one-dimensional, stained-glass saint: "Mr. Burrough was never much interested in politics. . .the last 21 years. . .one of the State Pilot Commissioners. . .only recently re-elected for another term. He was a thorough businessman and carried on all his work devoid of all display."

There is no doubt Burrough had a probably inbred, Yankee conservative style but the man's ideas about his work were dynamic. During his forties, the period of his letters to Aldrich, he was always thinking of new possibilities and didn't hesitate to reach for the greatest advantage he could get from whatever relationship he had with a man of great political power. In fact he asked Aldrich at one point to "say a good word" to President Benjamin Harrison about appointing Burrough to the position of Collector of the Port of Providence.

A significant difference between Burrough and Aldrich was that Burrough had a more narrow focus in his life's work: the advancement of Providence mercantile commerce, of bay shipping, and of a profitable role for himself in these overlapping areas. That was it, and he pursued that goal singlemindedly.

By the time Burrough had reached his mid fifties he was, within the local scene of Providence, taking up his own leadership in commerce and shipping without waiting on the power of the Great Man. In addition to the campaigns and successes mentioned above, he also campaigned to get the merchants who supplied rubber to Providence manufacturers to bring in the rubber by ship instead of rail as they were doing. In Chapter I we quoted from what was perhaps the greatest symbol of his leadership in Providence, the New Years Day 1896 petition he wrote to the Light-House Board about the lighted buoys with the 29 signatures of prominent individuals and organizations appended.

But Aldrich should also get the justice due him. While it appears to be true that in contrast to Burrough he was more interested in the profits of manufacturers and of his own investments, which he gained largely through his advantageous position in the Senate, and was devoted to the manipulation of political power for its own sake on a large scale, he was, at best, also dedicated to a role of creating balance and order, especially in commercial and monetary matters in Rhode Island, the United States, and the world. He is well known for his leadership in the negotiation of tariff legislation which balanced conflicting economic demands from across the country. He is credited with the ideas and planning which led to the creation of the Federal Reserve System.

Professor McLoughlin in his *Rhode Island, A History* says,

Aldrich realized that, if he simply looked out for his own constituents, he would pit himself in fruitless fights against other senators eager to aid their local interests. What American businessmen needed in Congress was a mediator, an honest broker, a man who could see all sides of a broad range of interests and harmonize the related needs of each for the best interests of all.

In trying to assess possible reasons for Aldrich's disdain for the idea of a light at Plum Beach in the early eighties we should keep in mind his sense of himself as a statesman. During the eighteen eighties Rhode Island industry certainly did benefit from his national leadership role in tariff legislation, and since, between 1882 and 1884, Whale Rock (partly through his efforts), Sakonnet Point and three other Rhode Island lighthouses were either built or had appropriations voted, it may well be believed that Aldrich did not want to spoil a good thing by overdoing it!

In a similar vein, Professor Sternstein has suggested that at the same time Burrough was petitioning him about Plum Beach, Aldrich was actively negotiating the location of the Naval War College to Newport, Rhode Island. Getting the War College was a far more important political accomplishment than the Plum Beach Light would be. Sternstein expanded on this theme in a recent correspondence with the author:

> . . . Because the battle over this issue was so important and difficult from Aldrich's perspective, it could be that to get the needed appropriations for the War College — which were always in doubt given the great hostility in and out of Congress and the Navy to placing the college in Newport — he slighted Burrough's request for the light station.

The austere budgetary philosophy of President Chester Arthur's administration is another consideration relevant to the timing of Burrough's two requests to Aldrich. The President vetoed the $19,000,000 Rivers and Harbors bill which the Congress passed in the summer of 1882. If that did not put a damper on Aldrich's ideas, it certainly must have put a damper on the already frugal Light-House Board, which, of course was part of Arthur's administration.

With Aldrich's aversion to putting his thoughts on paper, we may never find out whether he, in fact, knew a lot about lighthouses. However, if he was as well versed on that subject as on other technical ones, it may have been he was aware of the difficulties of constructing a light in the middle of the water. (See chapter III)

Until the development of the cast iron caisson lighthouse, it was technologically awkward and economically overwhelming to build waveswept lighthouses either on shoals or rocks in any kind of rough water in the icy northern climate. But cast iron caisson lighthouses used the kind of innovative technology developed for ships in the Civil War, that is, to produce pieces of iron that were cast large and thin and yet strong enough to bear weight and weather.

Robert L. Scheina, the U.S. Coast Guard Historian, in his *The Evolution of the Lighthouse Tower* has provided helpful explanations of methods that were used prior to the Light-House Board's adoption of the cast iron caisson method. In shallow water cofferdams were used. Made of wooden walls built on shore, then bolted together and sealed in the water, the cofferdams, after the water was pumped out, provided a relatively dry working area for construction to proceed. Construction in deeper waters, without the help of the cofferdam, was time-consuming and extremely expensive. The Race Rock Light (New York) was built in the 1870's by laying an interlocking foundation of five-ton stones upon five-ton stones — ten thousand tons in all, to the tune of a quarter of a million dollars. It took five years, and that was only the foundation!

Another type of waveswept lighthouse construction used before the time of the Plum Beach Light was the screw pile method of construction. Scheina explains that the lighthouse sat on top of wrought iron stilts "the legs of which are tipped with corkscrew-like flanges." The huge stilts were literally screwed into the ground under the water. However this type of construction would not withstand icy climates and fast running currents.

The Whale Rock Light, of 1882, and the Sakonnet Point Light of 1884, both built on rocks off shore, made use of the new cast iron caisson technology. Cylindrical pre-cast pieces of iron were built up, course by course, upon the rock base, then filled with concrete as they went along until the basement level was reached. Then, above the caisson, the superstucture of the lighthouse could be built.

However it wasn't until 1883, that any progress was made in the United States in dealing satisfactorily with the kind of challenge presented by the Plum Beach Shoal and other waveswept locations, where there were no rocks to build on and which were subject to rough, icy weather. In March of that year deliberations, unresolved over the previous year, about the building of an iron caisson light in one challenging location, finally became crystallized in the decision of the Light-House Board to build a new kind of caisson structure in the Fourteen Foot Bank Shoal on the west side of the main channel of

Delaware Bay. This would become the prototype of the pneumatic caisson lighthouse in the United States. After the Fourteen Foot Bank Light, ten other U. S. lighthouses, including Plum Beach, were constructed by this method.

In Chapter III we will take a detailed look at the pneumatic caisson method of constructing lighthouses, but here is a brief explanation of the method: a massive prefabricated wooden caisson topped with the first few courses of cast iron cylinder is lowered to the floor of the bay or river while compressed air is pumped through a sealed airlock into the hollow interior of the wooden caisson gradually pushing out the water and making it possible for workers to descend through the airlock and start digging. The caisson gradually sinks into the layers of shoal below the water insuring a solid foundation, which in the case of the Fourteen Foot Bank, was twenty-three feet below the top of the shoal.

By reading between the lines of Major David Porter Heap's definitive but modest 1889 book on lighthouse construction and administration, *Ancient and Modern Light-Houses*, we may conclude with reasonable certainty that it was none other than Heap who introduced the pneumatic caisson method of lighthouse construction into the United States.

We find the milestones and details of Heap's professional career in *Cullum's Register* of West Point Graduates published by its Alumni Association. He graduated from West Point seventh in his class of 27 in 1864; he served as an Engineer Corps officer in the Civil War building bridges and roads, making reconnaissances, making maps, repairing front line fortifications, and engaging in combat. Later assignments included improvement of harbors on Lake Michigan and serving as Engineer of the Tenth Light-House District from March, 1880 to June, 1881.

In August, 1881, Heap made his second trip to Europe — the first was from December 1870 to April 1871 — this time to represent the United States at the International Electrical Exhibition in Paris; then he went on leave of absence in Europe until April, 1882. This '81-'82 European trip was about the time initially disastrous attempts were being made off the coast of The Netherlands to establish the first known pneumatic caisson lighthouse in the unprotected, stormy waters of the Rothersand Shoals. Heap's blow-by-blow eighteen-page account, with careful diagrams, were to be detailed in his book. Heap's professional interactions at the Paris Exhibition were so thorough that a year after his return to the United States he wrote a technical report which included a chapter on lighthouses and which was published by the Army Engineer Department.

Upon returning to the States, Heap was given a ten-month assignment for Surveys and River and Harbor Improvement in Western Michigan. Then in March of 1883 he went to Washington to serve as Engineer Secretary of the Light-House Board. We reproduce here the first page of his Chapter XII, not only because of the attractiveness of it, but also because it shows what the Board was facing, the situation Heap found himself in when he got to Washington, and how he responded.

From the data available we make an interpretation: Before Heap arrived at the Light-House Board, discussions had already included the type of concrete-filled cast iron caisson that just sits on or just below the top of the shoal or the type which uses a hydraulic process to sink the caisson under its own weight. But no satisfactory conclusion had been drawn as to which was the more desirable. Heap arrived, fresh from the heady atmsophere of the European engineering scene where he learned much — perhaps from on-site visits. The size and importance of Delaware Bay and the difficulty of the problem reminded him of Rothersand. Perhaps during the two years of preparing the Corps' exhibits at the International Centennial Exposition in Philadelphia, he had conversed at John Roebling & Sons' dramatic Brooklyn Bridge exhibit, with Ferdinand or Charles Roebling. Their late father, John A. Roebling, had been and their brother Washington now was the designer and Chief Engineer of that bridge, which made use of the new pneumatic caisson technology for the foundations of its two massive towers.

In Heap's presentation to the Board, partially shown below, he does not say right out, "I persuaded them to use the pneumatic caisson method." He is not that kind of writer.

When he described the inviting of bids for the Fourteen Foot Bank Light caisson in December of 1884, he wrote with the same unassuming style: "Bidders were not restricted to any one plan for sinking the cylinder, but were allowed to use any process they pleased subject to the approval of the Board." He added that bidders had to "build and sink the cylinder so that its bottom would be 23 feet below the surface of the shoal." While it is possible to sink a caisson into a shoal to that depth without using the pneumatic method, it seems unlikely that any non-pneumatic method could insure its stability, given the nature of the weather on that bay and the nature of the shoal itself.

CHAPTER XII.

FOURTEEN-FOOT BANK LIGHT-HOUSE, DELAWARE BAY.

Fourteen-foot Shoal Light.

FOURTEEN - Foot Bank Shoal is situated on the west side of the main channel, about $3\frac{1}{2}$ miles from the Delaware shore, $10\frac{1}{4}$ miles northeast of the mouth of Mispillion Creek, and $14\frac{1}{2}$ miles north 51° 15′ west from Cape May Light.

This shoal, which is a turning point in the navigation of the bay, was marked in 1876 by a light-ship. Owing to floating ice, the light-ship could not remain at her station during the winter months, when it is very important to have the location of the shoal defined.

In 1882, the year after the disaster to the first caisson attempted to be placed on the Rothersand shoal, the Light-house Board of the United States considered the desirability of replacing the light-ship by a permanent structure, and several projects for the foundation pier were entertained. They all embraced the general features of a cast-iron pier filled with concrete. Different forms of vertical section for the pier were proposed and discussed; finally in 1883, a cylinder, 73 feet in height and 35 feet in diameter, was adopted by the Board, on the recommendation of Major D. P. Heap, Engineer Secretary of the Board.

This cylinder was to be composed of $1\frac{1}{2}$ inch cast-iron plates. 6

Major Heap is one of several individuals in the Corps, and in other occupations, who deserve posthumous honor for contributing to the cause of the Plum Beach Light. Later we shall see his more direct involvement in that project.

The budget appropriated by Congress for the Fourteen Foot Bank was $175,000. When it was finished, the job, had been done for $50,000 less than appropriated! This was an encouraging indicator of new possibilities for other difficult locations.

———————————————

If in 1882 and in 1884, after receiving requests from Rhode Island for action on the Plum Beach Shoal, Aldrich had pressed the issue, and if he had written to the Board with at least the same warmth he had used in 1882 when forwarding the Providence Board of Trade's requests for a lighted buoy near the as yet unfinished Whale Rock Light saying "I would respectfully urge the attention of the Board to the several requests," Plum Beach might have been the second pneumatic caisson light in the United States. Instead it was tied for fourth place with Smith Point Light on the Chesapeake Bay in Virginia. Even if Aldrich had known about the new pneumatic caisson technology in1884, it is doubtful that he would have made such a request.

What, in fact, happened was this:

Upon receiving Aldrich's late April, 1884 letter enclosing Burrough's second Plum Beach request, and including his own obvious put-down of that proposal, the Board immediately sent a letter to Captain George Brown, U.S.N. the Inspector of the Third Light-House District, directing him to report on "the advisability and necessity of establishing a light at Plum Beach." Brown's reply, almost three months later, with flourishes of language and script, attempts to provide the answer that is expected, given the prevailing budgetary, political, and technological climate, without entirely abusing the truth of the situation of the Plum Beach Shoal:

> I have the honor to state that, in my opinion, a light at the point named is not necessary.
> The Shoal at Plum Beach extends about five eighths of a mile to the eastward of the point but the channel between the point of the shoal and Conanicut Island is a half mile wide, with deep water close to the Island.

Dutch Island and Whale Rock lights are all the guides that are required to safely navigate the channel.

While a fog bell in the vicinity of Plum Beach Shoal would be serviceable in thick or foggy weather, this is the case at other points in Narragansett Bay.

It is practicable to establish a light on the point of the shoal referred to, but the expense would be very great.

> Very respectfully,
> Your obedient servant,
> Geo. Brown
> Capt., U.S.N.

Since Brown was the naval officer of the District and not the engineering officer, we would not expect him to be conversant with the innovative construction technology being planned for the Fourteen Foot Bank Light, nor, given the date, of the economy of that technology. (The total cost of the Plum Beach construction, when reviewed a few years after its completion came to only $69,989.62.)

At the beginning of this chapter we mentioned four characters who played significant roles in the story of the decision to build the lighthouse. We have heard at length from the Light-House Board, from Pilot Commissioner Burrough, and from Senator Aldrich; but we have not yet heard in this chapter from the Providence and Stonington Steamship Company, a subsidiary of the Stonington railroad.

An 1882 conversation with Senator Aldrich must have encouraged Providence and Stonington Agent Z. Williams to put it into writing, "Referring to our conversation I will mark down the needs of Harbor in the order of merit." And first on his list of four items is "Light House on Plum Beach." His needs are very straightforward and to the point. He ends

> These are important and I hope will soon be placed. Please use your best endeavors to have them completed at an early day and oblige

> Yours Truly
> Z. Williams Agent

He apparently is a man of few words. He is never heard from again by letter in this story and, like Burrough, he gets no action. The rest of the Providence and Stonington story, however, is not so straightforward; in fact, it is full of ironies.

The P. and S. had good reason to take the leadership it did in getting improvements in aids to navigation in the southern New England-New York waters. Any company which had had the disastrous season they had in 1880, for example, might be very nervous about the safety of their ships. Not only was there the public relations loss in the wreck of the *Rhode Island*, described in Chapter I, but far more serious was the loss of about thirty lives on June 11 of that year when their passenger steamer *Stonington* crashed into their passenger steamer *Narragansett* in foggy weather in Long Island Sound.

William L. Taylor, in his compendious study of the New England coastal steamship lines, *A Productive Monopoly* , tells us that the Providence and Stonington took a lot of criticism, especially from the magazine the *Nautical Gazette* and went through a federal investigation which only partially exonerated the company and its captains. Taylor also indicates that as a result of these accidents, steamship companies made a broad range of safety improvements, especially in the construction of new ships. From his information it would appear that the P. and S. , while making safety improvements on their ships, certainly did not take the lead.

When we see the pages of correspondence from the original president of the Providence and Stonington, D. S. Babcock, to Senator Aldrich in 1884 trying to get Congress to amend legislation about standards for construction of steamship boilers and to allow less stringent standards for a ship they are building on the grounds that it is a freighter that will not be carrying passengers, we may wonder how serious his commitment to safety was. It is one thing to ask Congress to appropriate money for aids to navigation; and it is something else to accept Congress' setting safety standards that require the company to spend more money!

We are told by an October 4, 1896 *Providence Daily Journal* history of the Providence and Stonington that Babcock, President of the P. and S. Steamship and Vice President of the Stonington Railroad, was killed in Stonington by a locomotive.

Babcock and the two future presidents of the P. and S., George Miller and J. W. Miller, wrote Aldrich on behalf of a number of corporate and personal causes. Of the two Millers the most interesting was J. W..

J. W. Miller, a native of Morristown, New Jersey, and son of a U. S. Senator, was a graduate of the U.S. Naval Academy. After asssignments in various parts of the world, the *Journal's* P. and S.

TERRIBLE COLLISION BETWEEN THE STEAMBOATS STONINGTON AND NARRAGANSETT,

Courtesy of Peabody Museum of Salem.

story tells us, he was appointed in 1873 to "special service in connection with the Nicaragua Inter Oceanic Canal survey." He later served as Secretary of the U. S. Commission to "determine which was the best route for a ship canal across the isthmus."

After discharge from the Navy, Miller served at an executive level for some midwestern railroads before coming to the Providence and Stonington as General Manager in 1886.

On February 4, 1889, J. W. Miller urged Senator Aldrich to push through a bill that would incorporate the Maritime Canal Company of Nicaragua, of which Miller would become Secretary, during the era when de Lesseps' prodigious efforts to build a canal in Panama were grinding to a halt. We can presume that Miller had money in the venture, and had perhaps taken a lead to get money from the P. and S. or other sources: "We have our two millions subscribed." His urgency to start construction had to do with the weather and with competition: ". . . various antagonistic elements are working against us there; notably deLesseps on the one hand, and the German influence on the other." Strangely, February 4, 1889 when Miller wrote Aldrich was the same date de Lesseps' French company officially came to an end in bankruptcy.

The newly incorporated American company started some work in Nicaragua, but by 1893 they too had gone bankrupt. The irony in this, for our story, is that the Light-House District Engineer, William Ludlow, who later made the greatest contribution to the success of the Plum Beach Light, was the same engineer President Grover Cleveland had assigned in 1895 to chair a three-man investigating board to inspect on site the proposed route, evaluate in detail plans and preparations made by the bankrukpt company, and determine the feasibility and cost of a canal there. The resulting report, described in detail by Ludlow's biographer, Eugene V. McAndrews, was professional in method and scathing in its portrayal of the technical inadequacies in the work done by the company Miller had supported so strongly in1889 and in the technical surveys with which the naval officer Miller was associated twenty years before.

But the Providence and Stonington was successful in the leadership it took in getting aids to navigation appropriated. In 1886 J. W. Miller, who at that time was the General Manager of the Company, sent Capt. Jones and Mr. N. I. Babcock to Washington to lobby for a lighthouse for Ram Island at the mouth of the Mystic River and west of Stonington, Ct. On July 2 George Miller, the President of the P. and S. writes Aldrich to thank him for his "kind and potent services" in getting the Board to reverse its decision against the "Ram Island lightship."

By 1892 J. W. Miller had been President of the Providence and Stonington for three years. It was a year that marked major turning points in the history of the Providence and Stonington Steamship Company and in the history of the Plum Beach Light. 1892 was also a bad year for the *Pequot* .

The troubles of the P. and S. freight steamer *Pequot* are summarized in a June 17, 1892 Providence *Evening Bulletin* article telling of the latest of its troubles that occurred on that day:

> The Pequot has met with a series of accidents during the past six months. In the early part of the winter she ran into barge John Hughes near Pomham Beach, knocking in the stern of the latter craft and damaging her own stern somewhat. Not long afterward she went ashore on Man-of-War Rock in New York Harbor and sank. Then she got afire at the Fox Point Wharf in this city.

With all due respect to the navigational difficulties caused by nature, such a record again raises questions about their commitment to safety. However, in the events of June 16-18 Captain Rackett of the *Pequot* was "exonerated" by witnesses, by the *Bulletin* writer, and by himself!

What happened to the *Pequot* this time? We are indebted to marine historian James Jenney for obtaining from a computer file the June, 1892 date so that the long, dramatically styled newspaper accounts could be obtained for our study. The heart of the June 17 *Bulletin* narrative reports:

> . . .The Pequot left the Fox Point wharf at 9:45 o'clock last night, having on board 69 carloads of freight. It was very thick and foggy, and the propeller proceeded down the bay at half speed. She went down the west passage and soon after getting by the half-way ledge the fog became so extremely dense that no lights or signals could be made out. The speed of the boat was reduced still more, but shortly before 12 o'clock, as Capt Rackett and mate Thomas were standing peering anxiously out into the baffling cloud of mist, straining their eyes to make out the familiar signals to the westward, there came a long smooth sound from underneath, the vessel seemed to heave herself out of the water, and Capt. Rackett knew that his steamer was ashore.

The immediate effort of Capt. Rackett to remedy the situation by reversing the engine was to no avail, and, later in the morning as the tide moved out, " the heavily laden steamer settled deeper in the soft sand of the beach."

Almost immediately after the grounding " mate Thomas with four of the crew manned a boat and after a hard pull he got ashore." The June 17 report says that the mate found that he was on Plum Beach. The next day's account, without explanation, located the beaching at Casey's Point, about a half mile farther south.

The mate "quickly made for South Ferry, which is connected with this city by long distance telephone [at Capt. Eaton's house] and summoned Agent Williams." Williams and Capt. Rackett ably coordinated the rescue effort which included temporarily moving some cargo onto schooners, getting three tugs to pull her off approximately twenty four hours after the beaching occurred, and having the hull checked for damage and leaks, before she steamed off again with cargo replaced, in a dry hull none the worse for all the excitement.

The June 18 *Bulletin* provides explanations "The channel of the west passage makes a long course from Warwick Neck to opposite Plum Beach. . .Capt Rackett had probably run on the outside of the Plum Beach Buoy [in 1892 not yet a <u>lighted</u> buoy] and when off Plum Beach about midnight, made out a schooner's light directly ahead. Presuming that the vessel was anchored near the channel as they often do, he attempted to pass her on the Wickford [west] side and ran squarely into Casey's Point head on."

And then the Captain's evaluation:

> . . .the great delay, and the expense in getting the boat off would constitute the greatest loss. . .his boat he considered, as practically uninjured. The unfortunate accident, he said, was one which is liable to happen to the most experienced coastwise sailor, under the circumstances which he encountered.

While we might think the explanation self-serving, we should also remember that radar was still about fifty years away.

The longshoremen give the *Bulletin* writer a similar opinion: "little blame could be attached to Captain Rackett . . ." And a local voice has the last word in the June 18, 1892 story:

> Capt. Arnold of Saunderstown says that the reach from Warwick Neck to Dutch Island is a hard one to follow foggy

nights, as a slight deviation from the course, or variation of the compass, tends to throw a vessel off her course unless lights are visible.

While the impact on the *Pequot* herself was minimal, the impact on Providence and Stonington President Miller was strong. On July 14, 1892 he wrote directly to the Chairman of the Light-House Board, Rear Admiral James A. Greer. The contents of the letter indicate that if Miller had not already been familiar with the Plum Beach situation, he must have made use of the intervening month to consult extensively. Very likely his consultation would have centered on the views of his own captains. It is reasonable to speculate that he might, either through his captains or directly, have consulted Pilot Commissioner Burrough and that he might have consulted Senator Aldrich in person. (No letters to this effect survive.)

Miller is assertive; so much so that when, by August 8, he had not received a reply to his July 14 letter, he wrote a quick note: "Dear Admiral, Did you receive my letter of July 14, a copy of which I annex hereto. Yours Respectfully. . ." Although readers of this book already know the information the letter conveys, we give the body of the letter in full because of the way Miller writes.

> Referring to the chart of Narragansett Bay which I send you with courses marked from Warwick Neck to Beaver Tail light. I would state that the navigation during fog from Warwick Neck to Dutch Island is extremely hazardous: our large steamers have had very narrow escapes from running on Plum Beach on the one hand and Dutch Island on the other. The distance from Warwick neck to Dutch Island is long and the Western Passage very narrow, and the lights at North Point [Conanicut Point at the northern tip of that Island] and Old Gay Rock are so distant that they are of no service.
>
> On behalf of the Providence and Stonington Steamship Company I would urgently request the establishment of some kind of a fog signal at Buoy #1 off Plum Beach. This matter has been agitated before, but the recent grounding of our Steamer "Pequot" off Casey's Point during a thick fog shows the absolute necessity of an aid to navigation between Warwick Neck and Dutch Island.
>
> I have had a thorough investigation of the above mentioned grounding of the "Pequot" which I shall be happy to show your representative, if necessary, at any time that he is in New York. I would further state that the presence of numerous schooners anchoring off Dutch Island add an additional difficulty of navigating the channel, especially during fog, and make it

necessary to get an additional bearing at Plum Beach, so as to avoid either shore in starboarding and porting off Dutch Island. The tonnage passing up and down the Western Passage is exceedingly large and the value of our freight alone per annum amounts to about $100,000,000 and the passengers during the five months which we run passenger boats during the summer is about 50,000.

The response following Miller's second letter to the Chairman of the Light-House Board was immediate and positive. Within a few days after the second letter arrived a copy was sent out to the Third Light House District. The response, written this time jointly by the District Inspector and the District Engineer, was sent back right away on August 25, 1892:

> We have the honor to state that a fog signal at Plum Beach would be a valuable aid to navigation and in view of the value of the commerce to be benefited, we recommend that it be established.
>
> As for its locality it will be necessary to build a secure foundation and a dwelling for the keeper we further recommend that a light be established as well as a fog signal, the additional cost of construction and maintenance will be small.
>
> The type of light-house recommended would be similar to the one under construction at Old Orchard Shoal, New York Bay and would cost $50,000.

The signatures under these few words that completely turned around the campaign for a lighthouse at Plum Beach were a study in contrasts: that of W. S. Schley a Navy captain who was District Inspector was small and barely legible; the second signature, belonging to the Engineer of the District, was done with sweeping, thick, firm lines — the first two initials being about an inch high and then a line continuing from the second initial swooping an inch and a half in each direction above and below the line into the first letter of the surname, *Heap.* It was D. P. Heap, the European-traveling engineer who had resolved difficulties over planning the Fourteen Foot Bank Light by introducing the pneumatic caisson method of lighthouse construction.

The next hurdle to get past was the Committee on Location. That committee made its report two weeks after the two district officers made theirs. The committee's September 8, 1892 affirmative letter paraphrased the gist of, and quoted some phrases from, Miller's July 14 letter with explicit reference to the *Pequot.* About a month later

CAPT. DAVID BABCOCK.

From *Providence Sunday Journal*, October 4, 1896.

Respectfully Submitted.

Captain...'Navy

Major of Engineers, Wachsman,
Engineer 3rd L.H. District

Conclusion of Third District August 25, 1892 report to the Light House
Board.

From the National Archives.

the Committee sent the Board another report revising the estimated cost from $50,000 to $60,000, " in view of the additional cost of public work due to the eight-hour law."

The 1892 Annual Report of the Light-House Board in turn made use of the committee's report for this portion of their list of recommendations to Congress:

> *Plum Beach, Narragansett Bay, Rhode Island.* The great Sound steamers plying between Providence, R. I., and New York, N. Y., find navigations during fog quite hazardous. In avoiding Dutch Island there is extreme danger of grounding on Plum Beach, as is shown by the recent grounding of the steamer *Pequot.* It is estimated that a proper light and fog signal can be established on Plum Beach for not exceeding $60,000, and it is recommended that an appropriation for this amount be made therefor.

The Annual Report to Congress for 1893 said the same thing, as did the Annual Report for 1894. Congress had not acted. No specific evidence has been found to explain its inaction. Perhaps it was the financial panic and collapse which began to grip the nation prior to the innauguration of President Grover Cleveland's second term in 1893 and continued seriously into 1895. Arthur Schlesinger, in *Political and Social History of the United States 1829-1925*, in explaining the complex causes for the financial collapse includes "lavish appropriations of Congress" near the end of the previous administration. Perhaps a backlash of thrift had overtaken Congress.

Apparently President Miller of the Providence and Stonington continued to put the pressure on for a lighthouse at Plum Beach, but now his pressure was on Capitol Hill. The Providence *Journal* article about the Senate vote on the Plum Beach Light on January 26, 1895 states, "The officials of the Providence and Stonington Steamboat Company have done their share in interesting Representatives and Senators in this important matter." Obviously an executive and financial leader of the national and international stature of Miller would have a lot more clout than a Chairman of Pilot Commissioners; and the interest in reviving the Port of Providence which bore such good fruit in the rivers and harbors legislation of the following year, had likely reached the ears of the Rhode Island delegation in Washington by 1895.

And so we discover in the *Congressional Record* for the session of January 26, that Senator Aldrich whose name has come up so often in

Number Key

1. Plum Beach Light
2. Plum Beach Point
3. Greene's Point
4. Rome's Point
5. Dutch Island
6. The Bonnet
7. Beavertail Light
8. Whale Rock
9. Narrragansett Pier
10. South Ferry
11. Saunderstown
12. Casey's Point
13. West Ferry
14. Wickford
15. Jamestown Bridge

Map showing West Passage and East Passage of Narragansett Bay, Rhode Island..

FromNational Ocean Service Chart 13221.

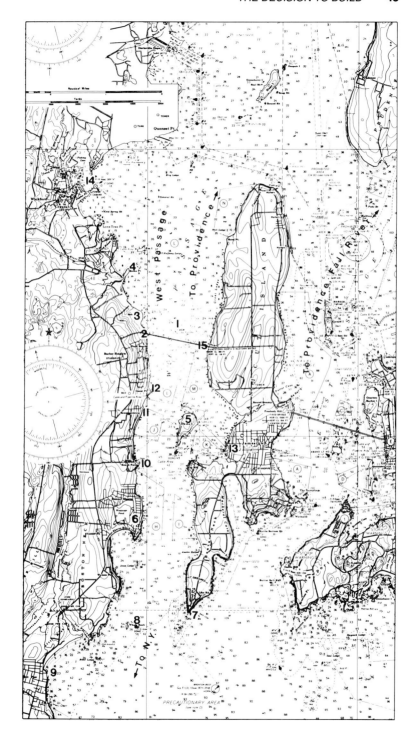

this story now speaks "for the record" on behalf of the Plum Beach Light:

> MR. ALDRICH. I ask unanimous consent to call up for present consideration the bill (S2565) for the establishment of a light house and fog signal at or near Plum Beach, Narragansett Bay, Rhode Island.
>
> There being no objection, the Senate as in Committee of the Whole proceeded to consider the bill.. . . . .
>
> The bill was reported to the Senate without amendment ordered to be engraved for a third reading, read the third time and passed.

The Providence *Journal* story the following day, part of which is quoted above, indicates that J. W. Miller and Frank M. Burrough were not the only people who wanted the lighthouse built.

LIGHTHOUSE FOR PLUM BEACH

Bill for its Establishment Passed the Senate Yesterday

The news that the Senate passed a bill yesterday for the erection of a lighthouse and fog signal on Plum Beach will be received with a great deal of satisfaction by every master who sails into Narragansett Bay.

It is in this locality that a situation from which a "departure" could be obtained has been so sincerely desired by navigators, particularly of those employed on the New York line of steamers. In passing through the comparatively narrow body of water off Plum Beach the pilots have hitherto been obliged to go more or less by guess, or more properly, by instinct, in thick or foggy weather.

All this will be changed after the erection of the station, and anxious owners, captains, and pilots will have a load of responsibility taken off their shoulders.

And the 53rd Congress enacted the legislation in the session of March 2, 1895.

A comparison of the history of the two neighboring lighthouses, Plum Beach and Whale Rock, provides a good summary of how decisions to build the lighthouses were made. First the differences: The initiative for the decision to build the Whale Rock Light was focused in the Congress. The letters show us that communication to the Light-House Board initially from Senate and House committees was as early as 1876. Senator Burnside in May, 1880 wrote the Board. Later that year, on the day after the wreck of the *Rhode Island*,

Aldrich, while still in the House of Representatives, wrote the Board a letter which has not survived, but which the index slip at the National Archives says was about the "necessity" of the Whale Rock Light.

The campaign for the Plum Beach Light, on the other hand, belongs to the shipowners, captains, pilots, and merchants. And the route of their success lay through the Light-House Board *to* the Congress.

But the two lighthouses also have something in common. In both instances a smoldering campaign was ignited by a steamship acccident: at least in the case of Plum Beach it is definite, and in the case of Whale Rock the minimal evidence turned up so far indicates that pattern.

We are now almost ready to proceed to the story of the construction of the lighthouse, but there remains one more irony about the Providence and Stonington Steamship Company: before the construction of the Plum Beach Light was finished, the Providence and Stonington, which had so ably championed the cause of the light, had ceased to exist.

The discontinuation of the company as an entity came about in 1898, as a result of complex transactions stemming from a takeover during 1892 and 1893 by the New York, New Haven, and Hartford Company of the New York, Providence and Boston Railroad which then had a controlling interest in the Providence and Stonington. During the 1890's the New Haven also gained control of most of the other southern New England Railroads and the other Sound steamship companies connected to the railroads.

We shall now turn to watch the steps by which one lasting monument to the twenty-three year old Providence and Stonington company and its enterprising president actually took shape in the middle of the West Passage.

III Construction 1896-1899

Heavy Labor and Integrity against Storm and Quicksands

"HUMP HER UP, boys!" Mr. Arthur shouted. "She'll start in a minute."

This was the second frustrating day of attempting to launch the Plum Beach Light, or to be more precise, the ten foot high, thirty five foot square wooden caisson, which would become the light's foundation, into the water in front of Hill's Wharf in Providence where it had been built. The contractor's supervisor, F. C. Arthur, was trying to encourage his crew.

The men in back applied pressure with two hydraulic jacks, and two screw jacks braced against the heavy timbers they erected for that purpose behind the caisson. In front, the slack tightened in the one inch wire cable running from a heavy upright post on the caisson to a heavy hemp cable which ran through pulleys to a winch. As the winch groaned the cable became taut in the effort to pull and push the almost 400-ton giant into the water.

If Arthur, his crew, and the large number of spectators who now stood on each side of the slip expected the caisson to proceed along the greased timbers beneath it with the glorious dispatch of a ship launching, they were disappointed. It moved only an inch. It was now the afternoon of Tuesday, August 18, 1896. Things had gone the same way that morning, as on the previous Saturday, when they had made the first try at moving the caisson. (Construction of the caisson had begun on July 13 of that year.)

Arthur and his men at the jacks and the engine tried again. This time, as the tension between the winch and the caisson grew, the taut cable began to break. They stopped again. Since Saturday morning the caisson had moved only four feet from where it was built. But now the cable was set up again, and The *Providence Journal* account on which this narrative is based tells us, "The men were pretty sanguine about getting it afloat while the tide was up." However, that was not to be: after they got the caisson to inch forward, rain came and ended their afternoon's work.

To get a better idea of what the caisson looked like and how it was built, we turn to a description of the American prototype of the pneumatic caisson lighthouse, the Fourteen Foot Bank Light in Delaware, written by the man who designed it, Major David Heap. Comparing his description of the caisson for the Fourteen Foot Bank with the engineer's plans for the Plum Beach shows that the caissons were almost identical.

> It was built of 12 x 12 inch yellow pine, and lined with 1 1/4 inch tongue-and-grooved stuff, laid in white-lead. The joints of all adjoining timbers were caulked and filled with mineral pitch; a sheathing of 2-inch yellow pine planks was placed on the outside. Work on the caisson was commenced on the beach at Lewes, Del., in the latter part of May, 1885; to facilitate launching the caisson in shoal water a temporary water-tight bottom was built. . .

The 12 x 12 timbers in the 34 foot square roof, or horizontal part of the Plum Beach caisson, were laid out one right next to the other, in four solid layers, of timbers of each layer running across, rather than parallel to, those in the next layer below. The four sides, 10' 8" high, were inclined outward slightly so that the base of the caisson was 35 feet square. These three-foot thick sides were also built of 12 x 12's, and the bottoms along all four sides were fashioned into two-foot metal plated cutting edges, whose tapered shape would eventually make it possible for the caisson, once settled on the floor of the bay, to assist in its sinking into the shoal itself as increasingly massive weight gradually added above forced the cutting edges deeper into the layers of mud and sand.

Built into the center of the roof of the caisson was a steel cylinder five feet in diameter and now extending about four feet above the caisson. Through this cylinder compressed air and workers, passing through an airlock, would, some weeks later, descend into the working chamber created by the inner walls of the caisson. Rising several feet from the top of the caisson were poles several feet high and later to be part of a framework, stabilizing the cylinder as its height was increased, with the first loads of concrete to go around the cylinder. During this week in August, 1896, the cable trying to pull the caisson into the water was attached to one of these poles.

SECTION.

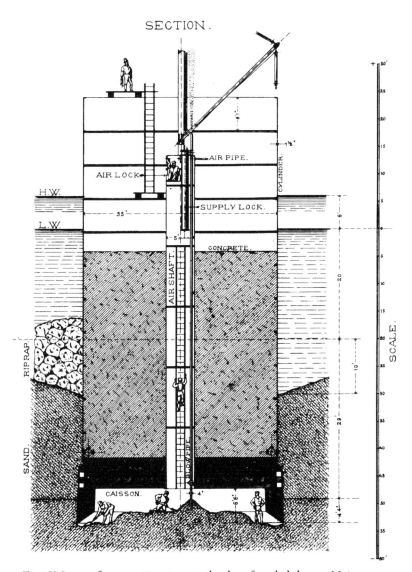

First U.S. use of pneumatic caisson technology for a lighthouse–Major Heap's innovation–at the Fourteen Foot Bank Light in Delaware, finished in 1886. Compressed air keeps water from flooding the work chamber, and forces the sandy debris up the blowpipe. While men dig, caisson being gradually filled with concrete sinks under its own weight. By 1896 at Plum Beach blowpipe was improved so that debris landed almost 200 feet from caisson instead of on top of it.

From *Modern Light-House Service* by Arnold B. Johnson. Government Printing Office, 1890.

Early in the morning of Wednesday, August 19 Arthur and his crew returned to this caisson hoping, on this third day of struggling, to send the 400-ton wonder into the waters of the Providence River. The *Providence Journal* articles about the launching explained that the difficulty was caused by settling of the ground which before construction had been built up with earth at the edge of the water. People familiar with the lighthouse over the years may decide that the problems in August, 1896 were prophetic of troubles that would plague the lighthouse throughout its history. However, on this occasion, as so often would happen in the future, there were people equal to the task who overcame the troubles.

After working through the morning moving the caisson forward inch by inch, the men took a break in the early afternoon and waited for the tide to come up. In the late afternoon when the tide was in far enough to cover the plates of the cutting edges on the bottom of the caisson, the *Journal* tells us, "the final effort was made. The heavy cables were strained until they creaked and the jacks were started up. Slowly the casing was pushed ahead. . .until the front part rested over the edge of the wharf, when the heavy mass slipped off with a big splash."

The reporter's description confirmed what the engineer had shown in his drawings: the displacement of the caisson upon launching would be so great that as it floated next to the wharf only a little more than a foot of the wooden caisson would show above water.

It would be close to a month before tugs would tow the caisson to its destination over the Plum Beach Shoal. There was still work to be done before the towing. We are again guided by Major Heap's description of the Fourteen Foot Bank, which corresponds with the directions contained in the drawings prepared in the fall of 1895 by Major H.. M. Adams of the Corps of Engineers.

The first thing to be done after the launching was to build upon the caisson the cast iron outer cylinder, 33 feet in diameter. Most of the cylinder would be built at the Plum Beach location. (This is the same cylinder the viewer today can see, the upper part fanning out in a trumpet-shaped curve to support the bottom of the lower gallery, 54 feet above the bottom of the cylinder resting on the wooden caisson).

Almost all of the cast iron plates were to be of the same size and design and were, therefore, interchangeable—a great advantage for construction efficiency. The plates were 6 feet high, three feet wide, and 1-1/2 inches thick. They had 6-inch flanges at the horizontal and vertical edges which had to be planed, so the joints after being coated with red lead could be bolted to each other and made watertight. The first course of six-foot plates going around the entire circumference were bolted down to the wood work, and the joint was caulked with oakum, a fibrous material used for caulking the seams of ships. Before the caisson left for Plum Beach the engineer's plans called for a second course of the six-foot plates installed.

There were three other tasks called for before the caisson could float down the bay: adding a few more feet to the *inner* 5-foot diameter cylinder to a height of about 13 feet, building up bracing for that cylinder and bulkheads to about 9 feet, and filling the space between the outer and inner cylinders above the caisson with about two feet of concrete.

When the wooden caisson with the new work on top of it was ready to leave Providence it would weigh approximately 405 tons and draw 16 feet of water.

At Plum Beach there was emerging a challenge more serious than that faced by Arthur and the crew in Providence. On the resolution of this challenge the safety of future occupants of the light would depend. The person who discovered and dealt with the challenge was Lt. Colonel William Ludlow.

Ludlow took up his new work as Engineer of the Third Light-House District in May of 1896. He was the fifth person filling the position of District Engineer within the space of two years.

One of his duties would be supervising the construction of the Plum Beach Lighthouse. Some of the problems that developed in connection with the construction of this lighthouse could be at least partly attributed to the lack of continuity in the unsettled leadership pattern of the District.

On June 11 Col. Ludlow wrote to Captain Black, Assistant to General William P. Craighill, Chief of Engineers in Washington, about putting off until the end of the fiscal year some responsibilities he had been directed to take on in addition to the Light-House Engineer assignment. It was typical of his sense of personal authority that he wouldn't take on the extra responsibilities until his predecessors had written their annual reports. During the summer of 1896 he wrote to the Light-House Board with what was essentially a courteously worded complaint about the Secretary of the Treasury's addressing communications about lighthouse business directly to him instead of going through the Board as the Board's protocol required. He knew how to stand and defend his own ground.

In the letter to Captain Black he said, "I have of course been greatly engrossed with this light-house work of which I had at once to take charge, finding much to be done and many loose ends to be caught up."

On July 9,1896 Ludlow on behalf of the Light-House Board signed a contract with the I. H. Hathaway Company of Philadelphia for the erection of the Plum Beach Light, including the building and sinking of the caisson and the superstructure above to the amount of $38,490. The contract did not include the cost of the cast iron for the caisson, and the cast iron for the superstructure made to the specifications of the engineer's plans in a separate contract with the Tacony Iron and Metal Company of Tacony, (Philadelphia) Pennsylvania.

Some of his work for the Plum Beach project was done by correspondence from his office in the Third District Headquarters at Tompkinsville, Staten Island, New York. However his most significant impact on the project happened during his extended on-site visits on the Lighthouse Tender *Mistletoe*.

In early September Ludlow made borings into the layers of mud and sand of the Plum Beach Shoal, lying 17 feet below mean low water, at the proposed location of the lighthouse, and at other locations in the vicinity. What he found disturbed him so much he sent off a report to the Light-House Board in Washington. The plans drawn up in November, 1895 by his predecessor, Major H. M. Adams, called for the wooden caisson foundation of the lighthouse to rest on a "hard bottom" 21 feet under the top of the shoal, or 38 feet below mean low water.

Ludlow found that immediately below that depth a stratum of fine sand made the ground very unstable, and that excavation would have to go down to approximately 43 feet below mean low water to find, as he said in a later report, "the stratum of fine, hard, and compact sand" upon which, in his view, the foundation could rest. Over the next three months Ludlow would continue to confront the Board with this problem which was both an awkward management issue, the contract with The Hathaway Company being based on Adams' plans, and a serious threat to the security of the lighthouse as a structure and of those who might occupy it.

Ludlow explained the structural issue in his letter to the Board on October 13, when the caisson had already been lowered to the floor of the bay, and additional courses of iron cylinder had been installed above the wooden caisson and more concrete added, but no digging had been done to sink the foundation:

The pressure on the bottom during the present weight in the structure, with allowance for displacement, is about one ton to the square foot, and with this weight which is about 1/3 of the ultimate weight to be borne, the caisson has already sunk nearly 4 feet into the bottom.

As this subsidence has taken place through the stiffest material to be encountered until the sand stratum is reached, there does not appear to be any reasonable expectation that the structure will be secure unless sunk to the full depth indicated by the borings.

What might happen if the construction of the lighthouse were carried out according to plan? At the least it might tilt under stresses like wind, or unequal weights above. It might sink down another 6 feet, either during construction or sometime later, which could cause injury to workers or keepers, and, since the high water mark would then be even with the drain pipe of the cistern and the cesspool, minor flooding would result on a regular basis, and ordinary winter storms and northeasters would cause serious flooding in the basement. The lighthouse would be essentially unusable. What would happen in weather conditions of disastrous proportions would be hard to say, except that it would be an extremely bad situation.

Why Adams had drawn the plans that way is hard to tell.

We do know that when Major Heap left the Third District Light-House Engineer assignment on November 5, 1894 no replacement had been assigned, a situation he complained about to the office of the Chief of Engineers in Washington on that day. Two days later Lt. Colonel Peter Hains reported for duty in that position, but in June of 1895 Hains "transferred" his responsibilities as District Engineer to First Lieutenant William E. Craighill, the son of the Chief. In that month young Craighill made the first drawing now surviving that can be conclusively associated with the Plum Beach Light.

Craighill's plan shows a cast iron caisson type construction without provisions for pneumatic sinking and without the square wooden caisson always used in the pneumatic process and sometimes used only to be filled with concrete to aid in sinking the non-pneumatic type of caisson construction. The depth of the water at mean low water corresponds with other engineers' description of the site, 17 feet. The depth of the bottom of the caisson below mean low water corresponds with the plans finally drawn up by Adams, 38 feet or 21 feet below the top of the shoal. There are some indications that a "hydraulic" method of sinking the caisson was contemplated.

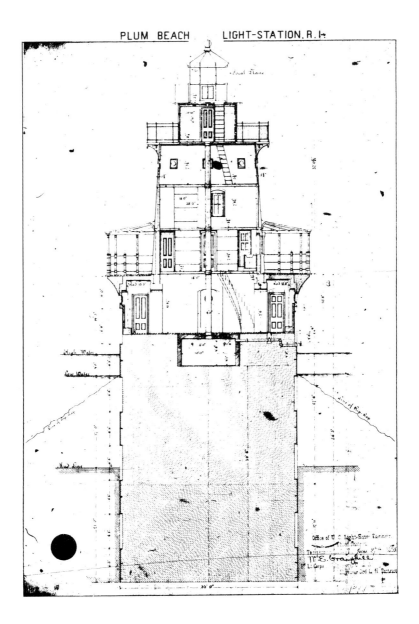

Lt. Craighill's June 1895 design.

From microfilm at U.S. Coast Guard Academy Library.

On October 23, 1895 Lt. Colonel Adams became Third District Engineer, and in the next months he drew up the plans for the Plum Beach Light. One page of the plans shows what is apparently cast iron caisson type of construction with what looks like the wooden caisson at the bottom just sitting on the top of the shoal with a very small amount (380 tons) of stone rip rap around it—not enough to keep such a structure stable. It shows a depth of 17 feet, which we know is the depth of the top of the shoal below mean low water. But in a later copy of the same drawing 17 is crossed out and changed to 21 feet which we know was the depth below the top of the shoal designated in Adams' final design. On "plate 1-1/2" of Adam's drawings we see the classic provisions for the pneumatic caisson type construction. The numbering of the plate suggests it was an afterthought. We do know that when Adams submitted his plans to the Engineering Committee of the Light-House Board in January, 1896, he got a response that approved them "with minor corrections."

If this all sounds confusing, it is because what actually happened was confusing. It was a government project!

Getting the proper data, proper analysis and interpretation of the data analysis is a pervasive problem in all kinds of public sector engineering. A casual study of the variety of influences involved in the 1986 *Challenger* explosion makes it very clear how complex the causes of an avoidable disaster can be and how critical the elements of personal and professional integrity can become.

Borings had been made at the Fourteen Foot Bank lighthouse site apparently after the lighthouse was designed but before the contract for building and sinking the cylinder had been drawn up. The borings, according to Heap, went down 26 feet, whereas the caisson was actually, according to him, sunk 33 feet below the top of the shoal.

When John Roebling presented plans for the Brooklyn Bridge in 1867 he made borings on the Brooklyn side of the East River to at least 96 feet, and had planned to leave the caisson for the tower on that side at fifty feet. On the Manhattan side he had bored through a lot of sand to find bedrock at 106 feet, and had envisioned the possibility of going down to 110 feet, exceeding any previous pneumatic caisson depth by 45 feet, according to David McCullough's *The Great Bridge*. The actual construction, under the direction of the designer's son, Col. Washington Roebling, brought the depth of the Brooklyn caisson to 45 feet, and the caisson on the Manhattan side to 78 feet, six inches. The data they had gathered before starting construction had been very helpful; yet even with all the helpful

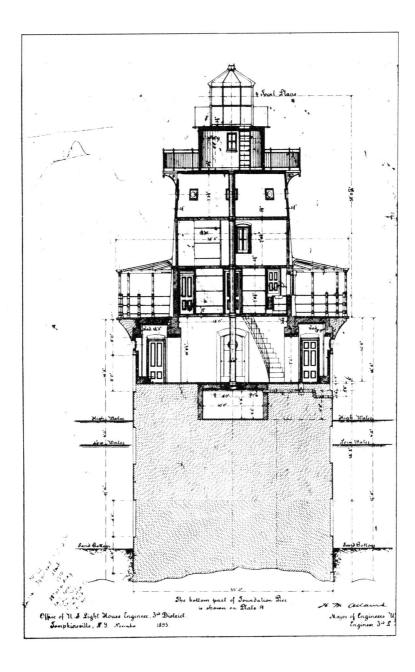

Major Adams' November 1895 design.

From the U.S. Coast Guard Academy Library microfilms.

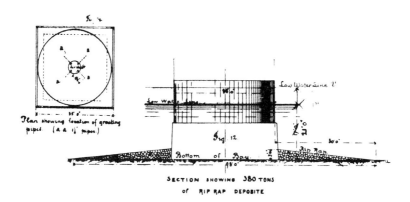

Major Adams' design for foundation resting on top of shoal. Even the correction seems in error.

From microfilm at U.S. Coast Guard Academy Library.

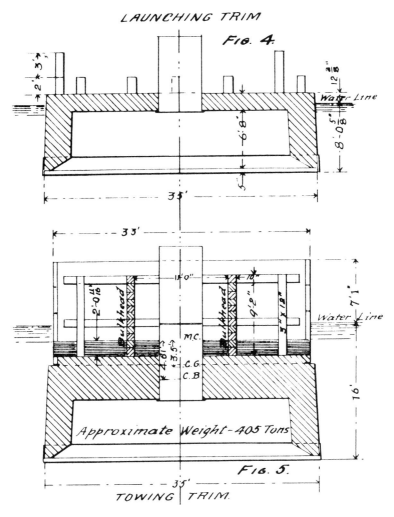

LAUNCHING TRIM

FIG. 4.

Water Line

6'-8"

35'

FIG. 5.

TOWING TRIM.

Water Line

M.C.
C.G.
C.B

Approximate Weight - 405 Tons

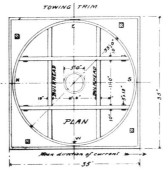

TOWING TRIM

PLAN

35'

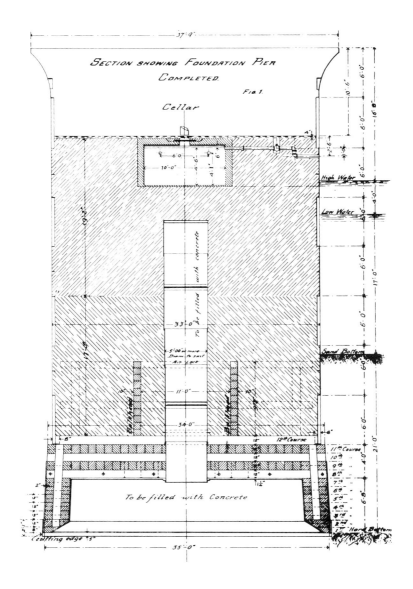

Major Adams' finished design for the foundation. "Plate 1-1/2." Uses D.P. Heap's 1883 design for Fourteen Foot Bank — a departure from earlier Plum Beach plans. Was it an afterthought?

From original at Governor's Island, N.Y. Courtesy of Engineering Branch, U.S.C.G. Shore Facilities Design and Construction.

boring and geological data they had collected, they still ran into surprises along the way.

While this book is being written, all is silent a few hundred feet south of the Plum Beach Light at the once busy site of the unfinished replacement for The Jamestown Bridge where work has come to a virtual standstill. The State of Rhode Island has an investigation going on to find out how and why it happened that only after the work of contractors was well under way they discovered that the design for the foundations of some of the bridge piers west of the main channel, on the Plum Beach Shoal, was not going to work.

The similarities between the Plum Beach Light problems and the bridge problems are interesting. Of course, to begin with, both are situated over the Plum Beach Shoal. In both instances a contract was signed and work begun without the benefit of some specific pieces of information about the engineering implications of the layers of the shoal.

However in the case of the Jamestown bridge, the proportions of the inadequacy were far more significant. Informal conversations by the author of this book with technical consultants indicate that more practical knowledge would have been garnered if *before* the bridge had been designed load-bearing test piles had been driven into the shoal rather than *after* start of construction. More importantly, if sophisticated, carefully controlled laboratory testing of the materials from the borings from the shoal were taken *before* the design was made, the designers would have had a better idea of how well foundation pilings would stabilize under the bay and what to expect in actual construction. Without seeing the results of the investigation we can at least hope that with the expertise available to bridge builders today, which was *not* available in the 1890's, the future progress of the new bridge will proceed successfully.

But such allowances for the difference between the 1890's and the 1980's being made, why was Adams apparently not concerned about the Plum Beach caisson depth while Ludlow was? It is hard to understand where Adams got the idea of a hard rocky bottom at 38 feet below mean low water. Borings taken for the new bridge (a sample report is shown in the appendix,) confirm in a general way the findings of Ludlow's borings of 1896.

Cullum's Register of the graduates of the United States Military Academy at West Point tells us that in 1866 Adams graduated first in his class. Many of his assignments indicate the rewards of brilliance. Within a year after graduation he had a two-year appointment as

Assistant Professor of Engineering at West Point; he was assigned as Assistant to the Chief of Engineers with a variety of responsibilities for many years; he served on boards, commissions and surveys too numerous to mention (he presided over some of them), and actually served as one of the part time members of the Light-House Board from June, 1893 to August, 1895. However, except for an early assignment as Assistant Engineer of Repairs for some projects in Mississippi, Louisiana, and Texas (1869 to 1874), his only assignments where he was actually in charge of construction were for a large number of improvement projects. His appointment as Engineer of the Third Light-House District, begun in October 1895 and ended in May, 1896 ran concurrently with many other positions.

Adams had never had a previous Light-House District Engineer appointment. Moreover, his tasks were chiefly focused in the office and conference room. Being an 1866 graduate of the Academy, he did not have the experience of having to make quick decisions under fire while doing construction near the front lines, as Ludlow and Heap had, during the Civil War.

To put it in the best possible light, he probably had many things on his mind with all these concurrent assignments. He didn't have the experience, and perhaps not the kind of inner organization of his own thought processes needed for making the kind of judgments Ludlow did.

William Ludlow was something else.

Born in 1843 (two years after Aldrich and Burrough) in Islip, Long Island, he came from families noted for their soldiers and political leaders. His father, William H. Ludlow, was both, having served in the Civil War with brevet ranks of Brigadier General and Major General, and later serving as Speaker of the Assembly of the State of New York. His grandfather, Ezra Ludlow, had been Architect of the University Building at the University of the City of New York, and in recognition of his grandfather's service Ludlow received a scholarship to study there.

Ludlow entered West Point at age sixteen in 1860. His biographer, Eugene V. McAndrews, tells us, he was "a young and impetuous maverick." In his first year he earned 202 demerits for misconduct; and his academic work did not show much promise either. McAndrews describes the situation:

> Whatever rule he could break, small or large, seemed his goal. Thayer [a previous Superintendent], early in his tenure, had forbidden drinking, card playing, gambling, tobacco

chewing, swimming in the Hudson, or leaving the post. Ludlow managed to taste every forbidden fruit many times over. And, of course, he was punished. Such was the code, although to many, the infractions were minor and the rules absurd. But it was the Academy's system, and would today be described as a generation gap. His first serious infraction was brazen. Smoking was forbidden. When the Chief of Engineers, General Joseph Totten, visited the post, Ludlow saluted him with a cigar in his hand. . .And he defaced many books for he was an avid reader; but he felt compelled to comment on their contents. . .

Although his rate of demerits remained high and although his misconduct would have disqualified him from graduation, the war was on, officers were needed, and his academic work had improved significantly over the years, and Ludlow was graduated in 1864, eighth in his class of twenty nine.

Ludlow served in the war with distinction. By March, 1865 the brevet promotions he had received for "Gallant and Meritorious Services" had brought him from the rank of First Lieutenant to that of Lieutenant Colonel. McAndrews tells us that Major General Hooker, after the Battle of Peach Tree Creek, recommended Ludlow's promotion "for gallant and meritorious service in laying a bridge across Peach Tree Creek under severe fire. . ." Later the many bridges he built across the rivers and swamps of Georgia made possible Sherman's March to the Sea.

Several assignments after the war became opportunities for military and engineering achievements that were solidly professional. Many were of a type that would make Ludlow ideally suited from a technological perspective, to be the District Engineer supervising the construction of the Plum Beach Light.

During the years he worked under Major Gilmore, 1867-1872, he had the assignment of "clearing of the Charleston, South Carolina, harbor and a number of inland rivers flowing into the Atlantic or Gulf of Mexico for ocean-going vessels." While in that billet he was commended for converting a rented steamer, the *Burden*, into use for "suction dredging" which could "remove ocean bars and was the first of a class of dredges which, in their later development, reduced both the cost of dredging and of river and harbor improvement," McAndrews tells us.

He was Engineer Secretary of the Light-House Board, from August, 1882, to March, 1883, and Engineer of the Fourth Light-House District for nine months in 1888. From December, 1888 to November, 1893, he worked in the Great Lakes region on a number of interrelated navigation assignments. During part of this time he was also District Engineer for the Ninth and Eleventh Light-House Districts, in which capacity, McAndrews tells us, he prepared a much applauded project for lighting the "difficult and narrow channels between Lakes Superior and Huron" and made night traffic possible for the first time. As engineer in charge of river and harbor improvement on the eastern coast of Michigan he effected changes in many harbors.

There was also the Chairmanship of the Nicaragua Canal Investigation Board, described in Chapter II, which kept him busy in Central America during May and June of 1895, and then for several more months writing the report. In the Spring of 1896 he was called to Washington for Congressional hearings on his report where he confronted engineers and others from the bankrupt Canal Company. The *Providence Journal* covered the hearings with articles and an editorial during April and May of 1896.

Four months before he made the first borings at Plum Beach, a May 5, 1896 *Journal* article reported that during the Congressional hearings Ludlow explained why survey data obtained by the Lull Commission of the 1870's and used by the Canal Company was inadequate:

> When the Commission returned to New York it found the information of the company regarding the bed of the San Carlos [River] to be utterly fallacious. It was taken from the report of the Low [Lull] Commission by which no borings had been made, a lead line only being used.

(It was the same survey on which the future President of the P & S, J. W. Miller, had worked.)

So the crisis at Plum Beach was not the first time Ludlow had to deal with a predecessor's failure to deal adequately with the earth underneath the water. Taking soundings with a lead line to determine water depths is quite a different operation from taking borings.

Speaking of the newspaper articles and Ludlow, it is interesting to note that in writing about the Lighthouse over the following ten months neither the *Journal* nor the Wickford *Standard* made the connection between the Ludlow of the hearings and the Ludlow of the lighthouse.

But what happened to the maverick Ludlow of West Point days? While Ludlow's military career was considered a distinguished one at the time of his death in 1901, he was still a maverick. It wasn't rebellious teenage escapades any longer but rather his ability to tell the truth as he saw it regardless of personal or political consequences and to fight like a scrapper for professional principles while still retaining his dignity.

Between 1872 and 1876 Ludlow was Chief Engineer for the Department of the Dakotas. We make use of McAndrews' detailed, strongly felt account of this appointment in his biography, and in his 1969 article on Ludlow in *The Military Engineer*. During a large part of this assignment Ludlow worked in conjunction with his friend and schoolmate from West Point days, the ill-fated General George Custer.

Ludlow held tenaciously to his views on several issues connected with the Dakota assignment. When he was asked to do reconnaissance expeditions in the Black Hills and in the Yellowstone Valley he wanted to make the expeditions not only good military engineering but also genuinely systematic scientific exploration of this new territory, and, to that end, he insisted on taking along with him civilian personnel professionally qualified for the task. Even more important were his views on U. S. policy and the attitude that Custer had about his (Custer's) mission. Ludlow communicated to Washington his disdain for Custer's, (and the government's) attitudes: cooperation in the commercialization and privatization of territory that belonged to the Indians by treaty and territory that should be preserved for the public to enjoy.

Ludlow understood that the Army had two responsibilities in the Dakota territory: protecting the settlers from Indians and protecting Indian lands from being overrun by settlers and entrepreneurs. The arrival of large numbers of gold-seekers would, Ludlow believed, abuse Indian treaty rights and spark an uprising. Ludlow argued with his old friend, Custer, and wrote candid reports to the Chief of Engineers in Washington against Custer's policy of baiting the Indians and seeking a fight with them. Fortunately, for the Plum Beach Light, Ludlow was made deputy district engineer of the Philadelphia area before his apprehensions about Custer proved true at the Little Big Horn in June, 1876.

Some of the political leaders in Philadelphia liked the work Ludlow did in that Corps of Engineers assignment so well, that in 1883 they obtained a leave of absence for Ludlow, with the help of Congress, so he could be appointed Chief Engineer of the Philadelphia Water Department. Again we take highlights of his biographer's epic account of the battles for reform which Ludlow undertook in this broadly conceived assignment, which included administrative management, scientific expertise and technical supervision, negotiation with political leaders and private contractors, and public relations.

With the Water Department Ludlow had many battles and he fought them all with vigor. He found the politics and business of the Department and the city as corrupt as the water supply was polluted. The only difference was there was a shortage of water! He even had to chide the Medical Association for failing to confront the serious danger and actual damage to the health of the people of the city which was caused by the pollution of the water.

The strong-handed integrity of Ludlow's reforms drew storms of opposition, and eventually the voices of the long entrenched establishment drowned out the voices of the reform minded politicians who had recruited him. He returned to military duty with a candid farewell.

Ludlow's candor and hardhitting persistence in dealing with thorny issues made his handling of the crisis of Plum Beach appear characteristic of his whole career. While he observed official courtesies, he did not hesitate to communicate in an authoritative manner to the Light-House Board in Washington.

However, one story about Ludlow's battle with corruption in the awarding of contracts in Philadelphia was probably more lasting than anything else he did there. It illustrates his wit, his sense of diplomacy and his integrity. We take the story directly from McAndrews:

> A contractor entered the office shortly after Colonel Ludlow's appointment to see about certain work. After some conversation he said: "Colonel, I suppose some of the boys want to smoke sometimes," and he laid a fifty-dollar bill on the desk. "Ah," said Colonel Ludlow, "you are a smoker. Have a cigar." Handing him one and taking one himself, the Colonel, talking all the while on other subjects, picked up the bill, folded it, lighted it at the open fire and passed it to the contractor. Both cigars were lighted and the remains of the costly spill tossed into the grate. The contractor's face was a study. But the lesson was effective.

But Ludlow could be sympathetic to contractors too; and this was evident in the very different circumstances at Plum Beach. When raising the caisson depth issue he was concerned about the security of the structure of the lighthouse as well as about unfairness to the I. H. Hathaway Company of Philadelphia. Whether he had known of the company, its owners, or F. C. Arthur, their superintendent on this project, during his years in Philadelphia we do not find out; but he paid attention to their concerns.

Since Ludlow had made it clear to Hathaway, as well as to the Board, that the lighthouse would have to go six or seven feet deeper than the 38 feet below mean low water called for in the contract, Hathaway, on October 9, presented his difficulties:

> If the Board should decide to have the extra work done, it is of the greatest importance that I be advised without further delay, so that the construction of the light house may not be delayed. If this work should be held back, necessitating keeping barges and men at light house site when the ice commences running, or if the work is stopped during the Winter months, it will certainly entail considerable extra expense, and the approximate figures given you by Mr. Arthur during the month of September would certainly have to be revised, in order to cover additional expense I may be put to. If there is any possible way to hasten the settlement of the matter, I would thank you to do so and now await your advices.

On October 13 Ludlow passed that communication on to the Board with his comment. In opposition to the bureaucratic inflexibility and penny-pinching policies of the Board, he stood firmly on the authoritative ground of his own expertise.

> The situation in this regard is sufficiently embarrassing to both parties, and Hathaway's desire, if possible, to learn at once if or not the extra courses will be ordered, is natural in view of the lateness of the season and the enforced prolongation of the work into mid-winter.
>
> If there be any way in which provision can be made for supplying the extra courses and putting them into the work, it would for many reasons be desirable to make disposition to that effect.
>
> As soon as the sinking of the caisson is begun I expect to make further investigation, but there is no reason to suppose that this will, to any material extent correct or modify the information already gained and furnished to the Light House Board in my report of September 12th ultimo.

He closes with the technical explanation, quoted earlier in the chapter, about the extent of "subsidence" of the caisson even without excavation.

Ludlow was caught between the Board and the contractor, and in this instance his sympathy for the contractor is clear. Communication between the Board, Ludlow, and the contractor continued over the next eleven days. The Light-House Board could not legally, and would not, order the added courses of iron plates, or work for which no appropriation had been made. They ordered

> . . .that the work proceed in accordance with the terms of the contract, and if it shall appear after having sunk the caisson to the depth stipulated in the contract, that further proceedings are necessary, the Board will then decide what action to take.

Now the work of sinking the caisson could proceed, even with a large question mark hanging over it.

Vessels passing by the eastern edge of Plum Beach Shoal during that autumn of 1896 saw a changed scene. Gathered around the construction site were either the steamer *Archer* or Saunders' steamer *Anawon* and a lighter, all carrying supplies, and the tug *Aquidneck.* The basic supplies for the project included the sand, stone, and Portland cement to make the concrete to be poured inside the exterior iron cylinder, as it was built up course by course, and around the inner 5-foot diameter cylinder.

A major part of the supplies would be enough of the 6' x 3' iron plates to build up the six more courses of the 33 foot-diameter cylinder on top of the two courses that had already been installed at the wharf in Providence. Then there was the coal to run the steam engines for the air compressors and water pumps. We include in the Appendix Engineer Heap's list of all the equipment used for the Fourteen Foot Bank Light, the foundation of which was so similar to the Plum Beach.

After the caisson was towed down the bay from Providence in September of 1896 and anchored over the designated construction site, it was necessary to extend upwards both the outer and inner cylinders, and flood the space between them with water until the entire caisson assembly would sink, under the weight, to its proper waiting place on the floor of the bay—on top of the shoal. Then the adding of stones would make it possible to pump the water out, and keep it down until the concrete was made with the stones.

This is the way things stood when Ludlow described, on October 13, how the caisson was sinking four feet into the mud and sand of the shoal under its own weight, without any excavation.

The next step was the starting up of the compressed air system connected to the shaft of the now sealed inner cylinder, and keeping the pressure on until all the water would be pushed out from under the 6'8" high, 29' wide working chamber inside the wooden caisson resting on the bottom. Clearing out that water would mean that workers could descend through the air lock. (it would hold several men at once) and then down the long iron ladder inside the five-foot wide tube into the work chamber below to begin the work of digging into the shoal.

From newspaper accounts we learn that there were twenty to thirty laborers ("navvies" in a *Journal* story) working on the project. The work was hard and under the worst of conditions. To get an idea of what working in a caisson was like, we cite David McCullough's description in *The Great Bridge* of conditions during the building of the Brooklyn Bridge foundations. First he quotes from E. F. Farrington, the Master Mechanic:

> Inside the caisson everything wore an unreal, weird appearance. Here was a confused sensation in the head, like "the rush of many waters." The pulse was at first accelerated, then sometimes fell below the normal rate. The voice sounded faint unnatural, and it became a great effort to speak. . .

McCullough goes on in his own words:

> Even the air lock was an unnerving experience for most men the first time they went down. For some it was also an extremely painful experience. . .Once the attendant had secured the hatch with a few turns of the windlass, the common sensation was that of being enclosed in an iron coffin. Then a brass valve was opened. "An unearthly and deafening screech, as from a steam whistle, is the immediate result," wrote one man, "and we instinctively stop our ears with our fingers to defend them from the terrible sound. As the sound diminished we are sensible of an oppressive fullness about the head, not unaccompanied with pain, somewhat such as might be expected were our heads to explode." (For many the sensation did not pass and they were said to be "caught in the lock.") Then the sound stopped altogether, the floor hatch fell open by itself. The immediate wish of most men at this point, whether they showed it or not, was to get back out into the open air just as fast as humanly possible. But once the ladder had been negotiated and three or four minutes had passed, most men also found they felt reasonably steady.
>
> The initial view of the caisson interior was generally something of a shock, once the eyes had adjusted to the light. The six big chambers [of the massive Brooklyn caisson] looked something like vast cellars from which a flood had only recently receded. . .covered with a slimy skim of mud. Every man in the

place wore rubber boots and got about on planks. . . and between the planks the muck and water were sometimes a foot deep or more.

It would be a very scary place to work, especially in the initial days of work inside the caisson at Plum Beach or any other caisson: If the compressed air system should fail, the loss of pressure in the chamber would allow water from the bay to seep in underneath and very quickly fill the chamber.

The crew worked with shovels probably by the light of paraffin candles in their hats, if we go by the experience of the Fourteen Foot Bank workers. Their job over the coming weeks was emptying the entire volume of mud, sand, shells and gravel from a 35-foot square area, 21 feet deep — that is, from the top surface of the shoal down to the depth the designing engineer had called for. As they loosened the material close to the perimeters, the cutting edges, carrying over a thousand tons of weight, would bring the entire structure, over their heads, deeper into the earth.

The debris produced by the digging was dispatched by a four inch iron blowpipe, a remarkable device which extended vertically from a point near the bottom of the working chamber up through the shaft above the chamber, all the way to the wooden platforms laid on top of the iron caisson a few feet above the water. The debris would be shoveled into piles around the bottom of the pipe, where a valve would be opened for twenty seconds at intervals of about a minute and a half. The force of the compressed air filling the chamber would, when the valve was briefly opened, send the debris up the pipe with a blast that carried the material a distance of 200 feet from the construction site.

The laborers might have been immigrants brought by the Hathaway Company from Philadelphia or New York, if we go by the evidence of similar construction projects of that era. If their workday was organized in a fashion similar to those who had worked on the Fourteen Foot Bank Light, they would have worked, as Heap describes, "in three gangs of eight men each, each gang working for eight hours, with a rest for meals after four hours work." The group of thirty men on the Plum Beach job rented a tenement belonging to Gilbert Willis near the foot of Main St. in Wickford.

The digging out, and the sinking, of the 35' square wooden caisson with the growing iron caisson on top, continued until December 5. The cutting edge of the caisson had reached 35'3" below mean low water—just 2' 9" above the 38 foot permanent depth

On top of cast iron caisson of the Fourteen Foot Bank Light, Delaware Bay,
during the sinking of the caisson. Hose from Morro Castle hull brings
compressed air through airlock device down into base of caisson. Worker is
clearing debris from the excavation which the exhaust pipe has thrown on
top of airlock and on the temporary working platform across
top of caisson.

National Archive photo.

called for in the contract; they had come down through 18 feet of mud, sand, and shells below the water. During December 5th and 6th Engineer Ludlow made a boring from inside the southwest corner of the chamber.

The boring showed that 1'6" below the present level of the cutting edge lay a 6' 9" stratum of quicksand. The *Journal* article on the problems about the depth of the caisson says Ludlow "at once ordered Mr. Arthur to suspend operations. . .". Given the uncertainty about what, if any, changes in plans the Light-House Board would authorize, it was safer to leave the caisson where it was, at least temporarily, midway in a stratum of coarse sand, than to proceed any further into the quicksand.

In his December 7 letter to the Board, which he wrote on the tender *Mistletoe,* Ludlow is more low-key about the ceasing of operations:

> Pending decision as to the means to be adopted to ensure stability to the structure the Contractor has of necessity suspended work and now awaits further instructions as to how to proceed.

Twice in this letter, in almost the same words, he points out that he gave them prior warning:

> The information obtained verifies the borings made in Sept. and fully detailed in my report of Sept 12, with the addition, from actual samples, that some of the material passed through, and indicated as "fine sand" is in fact quicksand.

(Armand J. Silva, Professor of Ocean Engineering of the University of Rhode Island has advised the author that the difference in boring results of September and December, i.e. that quicksand appeared in December, probably resulted from water of the bay being introduced into the stratum by the entry of the caisson into the shoal.)

One of the differences between the 1890's and the 1980's is the greater rapidity in the early days of mail communication between Providence, New York, and Washington. Ludlow wrote the Board on December 7, 1896, got a reply on the 9th, and sent off his response with the proposal the Board had requested from the contractor for "sinking the caisson below the contract depth, and making other provision to secure the structure until such time as further steps can be taken to complete it — on condition that all compensation to

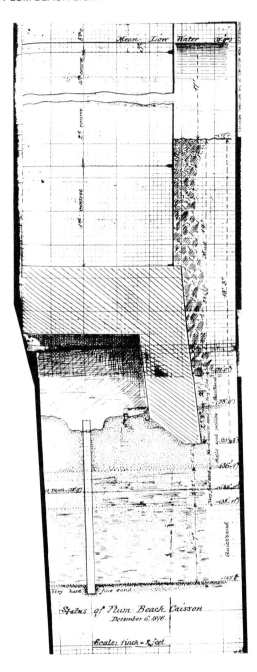

Lt. Col. Ludlow's sketch of borings taken from inside the caisson on December 6, 1896, verifying the bad news of his September 12 borings.

contractor be within the amount now stipulated in his contract, to wit, $38,490."

The *Providence Journal* writer makes the story more dramatic than we can assume from the correspondence now available:

> . . .Lieut. Colonel Ludlow, accompanied by the contractor, paid a visit to the headquarters of the Lighthouse Board in Washington, and the state of affairs being laid before them, the members decided that the caisson with its cylinder must be sunk an additional seven feet to the sand bottom.

The correspondence indicates that by December 8, after reading Ludlow's report, the Board, or at least the Engineer Secretary of the Board, was open to revising the contract to save the lighthouse as long as no extra money would be spent.

In response to the Board's request for a new proposal, Mr. Arthur wrote on behalf of the Hathaway Company:

> If advised to proceed at once I will sink the caisson of Plum Beach Light House seven (7) ft. four (4) inches below the present contract depth, fill the working chamber and air shaft with concrete as per present specifications, place the two (2) courses of iron now at the site viz. Nos. 7 & 8 on cylinder, fill the seventh course of plates to the top with a ring of concrete extending full way around inside of cylinder plates, five (5) feet wide at bottom and three (3) ft. wide at top as per sketch furnished and fill inside of same with sand — sand can be removed by you at your pleasure — I also agree to put a rough covering over the 8th course and brace same course as per direction of Engineer in charge. Also to place iron covering over outlet holes in cylinder plates as per directions of Engineer. When this extra work is completed I am to be paid in full ($38,490) same as if the contract had been carried out as per my original agreement and am to be relieved of all future responsibilities.

The bell-shaped eighth course of cylinder plates would now be installed and at a later time, when the extra ninth course would be procured, under a new appropriation, would be removed and then placed on top of the new plates.

We will probably never find out whether the *Journal's* more dramatic story of Ludlow and Arthur hurrying to Washington to present before the Board really happened. If it did happen it would have had to have been between December 9, when Ludlow forwarded Arthur's letter, and December 14 when the Light-House Board wrote to their ex-officio President, the Secretary of the Treasury, about the Plum Beach situation. If it did happen, it might explain why the December 9 letters were logged in at the Board's office as received on the same day. In any case the chronology in the Appendix contains information on the functioning of the Board which is at variance with the official correspondence.

The Board agreed with the Hathaway Company's proposal written by Arthur, and directed Ludlow to sign a supplemental agreement with him. The letter sent to the Secretary of the Treasury by the Engineer Secretary of the Board indicates the extent to which they wanted to downplay the difficulties in the original plans. If there were difficulties in the transactions between the Board, the Third District Engineer, and the contractor, to the point that Ludlow and Arthur actually had come to Washington, no one was going to let on.

> The Board has the honor to state. . .
>
> It now appears that the interests of the government require certain modifications to be made in the specifications for this work to meet conditions which were not known when the contract was made. . .
>
> The Board therefore obtained an offer from Mr. I. H. Hathaway, the contractor as to the terms. . .
>
> The Board is of the opinion that it is to the interests of the government to have the specified work done. . .and therefore directed the Engineer of the 3rd Light-House District under the date of 9 Dec. '96 to take the necessary measures to enter into an agreement. . .
>
> The Board now has the honor to ask approval of this action . . . .

According to the protocol of the Light-House Establishment it was necessary to ask the approval of the Secretary of the Treasury, the President ex-officio, of the Board, who according to custom rarely met with them. The Engineer Secretary in his letter enclosed some correspondence: the December 9 letters of Ludlow and Arthur and the Board's response. Perhaps the truth of the story lies somewhere between the more dramatic newspaper version and the low-key everything-under-control (our control) officialese of the Board.

So the final stage of sinking the caisson continued, and by the fourth week of January, 1897 the cutting edge, with 2900 tons bearing down on it, and with the laborers sending their last piles of debris up the blowpipe, reached its final resting place at 45 feet below mean low water. The working chamber at the bottom of the five-foot wide shaft was filled with concrete.

Some of the workers headed for home, and the steamer *Archer* began hauling the equipment used in construction to Wickford, where it was loaded on a barge to be carried to New York. By noon on February 1 all the workers had left. January 31 marked the end of F. C. Arthur's work at Plum Beach. Arthur bid as an independent contractor for the second contract of the Plum Beach Light in 1898, but was underbid by a competitor. Somehow he kept his name prominent in lighthouse construction. Twenty one years later when more construction at the Light was being discussed, it was recalled that Arthur had represented the contractor during the first contract.

Several things remained to be done. Col. Ludlow had been concerned about the riprap that would be placed around the caisson. *Riprap* is a term referring to rocks, in this case approximately 4 tons apiece, which would be laid around the the base of the lighthouse to help keep it steady. Adams' original drawings called for 380 tons of riprap. The subsequent original contract with the suppliers of the riprap called for 1500 tons, at a cost of $2,100. Ludlow wondered whether perhaps another 2,000 tons should be added to that, because "the total height of the structure is increased by eight feet, correspondingly increasing the leverage of the ice and current forces tending to overturn the structure." Since Ludlow acknowledged he wasn't sure about this (contrary to his firmly held opinion about the caisson depth) apparently the Board did not take the issue seriously. The steamer *Archer* began taking the 1500 tons of riprap to the lighthouse foundation in February, and more was brought in October, 1898. However the riprap added in 1897 and 1898 is not that visible at the base of the lighthouse today. The original riprap only came up at its highest to a few feet below mean low water. The riprap now visible was added in 1922.

Official statistics about the Plum Beach Light usually state that it was "built" or "established" in 1897. Considering how much there was still left to be done when F. C. Arthur finished off the Hathaway Company's obligations the designation of 1897 as the year of record may seem strange. However, the Plum Beach Light as a working beacon was established in that year. This is how it happened:

The Hathaway Company, after filling in a protective load of sand on top of the concrete interior at the top of the iron cylinder, had placed a wooden roof across the top of the unfinished cylinder, and painted it black. An upright spar was established in the center of the roof, and a red lantern light was hung from an arm extending from that spar. And this is where Capt. J. Lester Eaton comes into the story of Plum Beach Light. Commander A. S. Snow, the Inspector of the Third District, asked the Board to employ Capt. Eaton as "Acting Keeper." The Acting Secretary of the Treasury authorized the hiring of "a Laborer" at $20. per month. Capt. Eaton continued to row or sail out to the unfinished light every day until it was completed, with the exception of periods when actual work was being done on it.

There was no debate about the need to establish the temporary light. If the Shoal presented a hazard to mariners, certainly the unfinished hulk of the iron cylinder *unlighted* would provide a greater hazard. However, J. W. Miller, President of the Providence and Stonington Steamship Company, wanted more than a light. Miller, in his last letter to the Board about Plum Beach on February 15, 1897, uses almost the same language he had used a few years before to argue for the establishment of the lighthouse:

> . . .the caisson is right in the track of our steamers, and in case of fog is a dangerous obstruction. Our captains, by giving it a wide berth in thick weather, are liable to run on shore on the Dutch Island side of the channel.
>
> I therefore, respectfully ask, if consistent, that some kind of fog signal be placed on the caisson. . .

Both the Third District Officers, Snow, the inspector, and Ludlow the Engineer concurred in rejecting that proposal, because there was no shelter for a keeper to tend it, and they could easily have the former bell buoy in the vicinity replaced. However, in this instance, the people in Washington outdid Ludlow in their concern for safety, or for Miller. Comments on the face sheet of the letter include, "I do not agree with the D. O's [District Officer's] conclusion. Caisson is a serious obstruction to navigation," and from the Engineer Secretary of the Board, "If nature had provided a rock in or about this place we would not wait long to put a signal of some kind on it."

The District Officers were overruled. A fog signal, a 1,028 pound bell struck by machinery, a double blow every 30 seconds was installed with the temporary light on June 1, 1897. In March of the following year Engineer Heap arranged for a shelter so that Eaton could stay on the unfinished light when fog was coming.

Essentially, at the end of February, 1897, the revised contract with Hathaway had been fulfilled; the iron work already prepared for the superstructure was lying in storage in the Tacony Company's yard at Philadelphia, and the temporary light, later to be joined by the fog signal, was being tended by Eaton. The Board in its Annual Report to Congress reviewed the construction history of the light briefly, and recommended appropriation of $9,000 to complete the job.

As happened so frequently in the news stories of that era the author of the long *Journal* report of February 8, 1897, which we have used in this chapter, ended with an "editorial": "It is hoped that this Congress will take action on the subject, as the establishment of a beacon at this point in the West Passage has already been long delayed."

In March, 1897 Ludlow was transferred to responsibility for harbor channels in a large area in and around New York Bay.

During the next year and a half, lighthouse tenders *Rose, Cactus,* and *Mistletoe* came in and out of the West Passage for a variety of small jobs which included moving buoys, establishing the fog bell next to the temporary light, and tending to other lighthouses.

In April of 1898 the United States went to war with Spain. As would happen in the two following wars, this one had a marked effect upon the Narragansett Bay. In the first week of May, Newport harbor and the East Passage were "closed to navigation from dark to dawn," the Wickford *Standard* reported. The following week the West Passage was mined, and no vessels could pass between 8:00 p.m. and 4:00 a.m.; but in the third week of May lighthouse tender *Cactus* put down some buoys to mark a channel, and in the evenings "a government vessel" piloted the Providence steamers through the minefield.

In June Brigadier General William Ludlow went to Cuba. Later, because of political infighting between his superiors, there would be controversy over Ludlow's many and varied activities in Cuba. Trying to overcome a woeful lack of preparedness on the part of the Army, he labored to organize for the arrival of U. S. troops. He was commended for bravery in leading a brigade in the battle of El Caney. Eugene McAndrews, in his *William Ludlow; Engineer, Governor, Soldier*, which has provided so much of our information about Ludlow, quotes from a letter from Ludlow to his daughter. In it Ludlow interprets his experience at El Caney in religious terms:

> All through that day of desperate work at Caney I was aware of a means of protection that left me without any apprehension for my own safety and since then I have been much the same.

McAndrews adds his own comment: "Ludlow was convinced that he could not or would not fall in battle."

After the war Ludlow joined other officers in demanding early evacuation of troops after an outbreak of yellow fever which spread through the troops. He too had suffered from fevers during the campaign. He complained in person to Secretary of War Alger about the unsanitary condition of troop ships which also carried cattle. On December 13, 1898 the President appointed Ludlow Military Governor of Havana, where he labored diligently to restore some order in the midst of chaos. His comprehensive administration of municipal rehabilitation of Havana gave special attention to the unsanitary conditions which contributed to widespread illness there. Even though he had gotten along well with Cuban army officers during the war, and even though he had encouraged cordial social relationships and the rudiments of democratic process as Military Governor, the strong-handed direction he gave in many areas caused strong opposition by Cuban newspapers and some political leaders.

In March of 1897 Ludlow's West Point classmate, that man of the modest words and stunning signature, the American developer of the pneumatic caisson, Lt. Col D. P. Heap, succeeded Ludlow as Third Light-House District Engineer, a position which Heap himself had held from 1887 to 1894. A year later he arranged for a shelter on top of the unfinished Plum Beach structure so that Capt. Eaton could stay there to operate the fog bell when necessary. In his letter to the Board about his plans Heap concludes wistfully that the "station will never be a satisfactory aid to navigation until [a] tower is built."

Finally on July 1, 1898 Congress appropriated $9,000 to complete the Plum Beach Light, and Heap began the process of bidding and negotiating a contract for the creation of the lighthouse tower on top of the iron caisson.

In contrast to the 1896-97 construction story, which might well be characterized "the engineer's story," the 1898-99 episode is really "the contractor's story".

Heap informed the Light-House Board that the bid of Toomey Bros. of Guilford, Connecticut, of $8,420 was reasonable, but that he had persuaded that company to reduce their bid by $587, because the original bid along with the other costs budgeted would have brought the total outlay over the appropriated amount. By September 23 the iron plates for the additional cylinder course, necessitated by Ludlow's sinking of the foundation caisson an extra seven feet, had already arrived under a separate contract on a dock in Newport, ready to be used, and Heap chided the Board for not acting on the information he had sent on the bids.

In fact Engineer Secretary Millis had on September 21 written to the Secretary of the Treasury for approval of the bid, and on September 23 Millis wrote Heap and told him to go ahead and make a verbal agreement with Toomey Bros. to start the work immediately pending the execution of the contract. And the Friday October 14, 1898 the Wickford *Standard* duly noted that a schooner was seen making preparations and that work began "last Wednesday."

After installing the extra course of cylinder plates the Toomey people had a long wait because Tacony failed to send the iron work for the superstructure of the lighthouse on time. The iron work, already paid for during the first contract, and stored in Tacony's yard in Philadelphia, was expected on November 19, but Tacony argued for sending it to Providence rather than to Newport, as indicated in the Tacony contract. Perhaps the disinclination of Toomey to pick up the iron from a wharf in Providence, contrary to the contract, was intensified by the fact that Toomey was using a schooner rather than steam vessels such as Hathaway had used, and they would probably need a tug to pull the schooner through the narrow channel of the Providence River.

This delay presented a great burden to the contractor. Toomey wrote D. P. Heap,

> Colonel: We wrote to the Iron Company some time ago to hurry the iron along for Plum Beach Light-House. Now the iron is not here, and I am under the expense of $40. per day while we will be delayed, as we were ready to go after it this afternoon with schooner. I also telegraphed them to hurry it along.

And then there was the weather. During the last weekend of November, 1898 came the storm which William P. Quinn in *Shipwrecks Around New England* called " the most dangerous storm of the decade," and the storm that "wrecked more ships [140 by his count] than any other in the history of New England." It has been called "blizzard," "hurricane," and "gale," and began on November 26. Quinn describes it:

> The blizzard raged at full intensity for thirty-six hours, gradually abating on the third day. Seventy mile per hour winds lashed the entire New England coastline. The seas became higher as the storm gained in intensity. The oceanic turbulence tossed ships on shore like driftwood. The most noted wreck during the gale was that of the steamer *Portland* lost with all her crew and passengers. It was estimated that between 150 and 200 people were aboard when she foundered somewhere north of Peaked Hill Bars off Cape Cod.

After many pages of the 1880's and 90's *officialese* used by most of the letter writers quoted in this and the last chapter, H. Toomey's letters are refreshing in their directness. In his December 3 letter to Col. Heap Toomey told how the great November storm affected the crew at Plum Beach:

> We thank god that all was not lost at Plumb beach R. I. in the blizzard Saturday night, as there was only one chance out of a thousand. The schooner [Beattie] dragged from Plumb beach out to beavertale where she got foul with her anchor in a torpedo cable and held on. If she wasnt a strong boat she would be smashed.
>
> Col. in case the weather gots to bad & we cant work, can we please stop the work for 90 days at Plumb beach, Narragansett Bay is the stormiest place we ever worked. It is either raining or blowing half the time.
>
> Very truly yours,
TOOMEY BROS. & CO.
H. Toomey

Apparently the Light-House Establishment typist, who later copied this series of letters, also appreciated the writing and the grammar of this man whose ideas were so straightforward and clearly expressed. In his January 9,1899 letter he presented with greater seriousness, and with the same narrative vigor, the specifics which made it impossible for Toomey Brothers to complete the construction of the lighthouse by the contract deadline of February 10.

> . . . almost continuous fight with the elements no work could be done on 21 working days of the whole number of 66 we have been here up to Dec. 24th. . .the station is very dangerous and difficult of access in stormy weather and in the present condition it is not habitable for workmen we have been unable to innge carpenters at any price to do the carpenter work at this season of the year and it was with great difficulty that we could retain the bricklayers long enough to finish the cellar its also a question whether the painting can be done properly at this time we propose to close the tower against the weather & store the remainng iron safely, and would like to suspend operations until April 1st, 1899. . . .

In Engineer Heap's January 28 letter to the Board we see clearly laid out what a sad and dishonorable story this is: After receiving Toomey's strongly felt December 3 letter right after the Blizzard, Heap had written Toomey to make a "special application for stopping work." Heap apparently understood Toomey's January 9 letter to be that application, and on the 12th he recommended to the Board that the contractor have "an extension of time on their contract."

By January 17 the Board had still not replied to Heap's recommendation, and Heap withheld any approval of the request. Toomey, having had enough, closed down the operation and left until better weather should arrive.

Heap, like Ludlow, was a man caught in the middle. It is no wonder that by 1910 Congress and President Taft wanted the Light-House Establishment reorganized with a single national authority the Commissioner of Lighthouses, delegating substantial authority to District Superintendents. But Heap, in 1899, caught in the middle, informed Toomey that "in the absence of any authority. . .they must assume all responsibility for their action." He was a fairminded man, and represented accurately to the Board the "due diligence" of Toomey; but unlike Ludlow, he did not take a stand in opposition to the way the Board treated the contractor.

Perhaps there is another dimension to this sordid business. The stationery of the Tacony Iron and Metal Company, containing the picture of their plant, several acres of large factory buildings with tall smokestacks billowing smoke and with ships at the dock beyond presents a picture of corporate power. With all the fuss they raised about the difficulties of shipping to Newport instead of Providence, Tacony probably had the office staff and the profit margin to organize and pay for the routing of the iron to Newport. The Board was staffed with representatives of political and military power. But at Plum Beach you had, not the Philadelphia contractor, Hathaway, but Toomey from the village seaport of Guilford, Connecticut, with his writing style suggesting humble origins, and who had probably kept his bid low by personally doing his own supervising and using a schooner instead of steamers: "It doesn't really matter how we treat this little guy," might easily have been the Board's attitude.

On February 13 an extension to the contract was agreed upon. In the spring, work was resumed and the lighthouse was finished by June 1, 1899. The next document available to us in the National Archives regarding the relationship between Toomey and the Board comes in 1905. It is a letter from Toomey Bros. & Co. to the Engineer of the Third Light-House District; and unless H. Toomey had been to night school in the last five years, it is by a different author. The letter recounts the difficulties of the delay in delivery of the iron works and the severity of the weather. The letter concludes:

. . .Had the iron been delivered on time we would have been able to close in the tower and finish the Light-House on time and have been spared the loss caused by the 17 days of delay which we place at $100.00 per day or $1700.00.

This amount, together with the amount of the penalty exacted from us $1631.20 making a total of $3,431.20 we ask you to pay.

The District Engineer pulled out of his files 29 letters from 1898 and 1899 and found that the only charge against the Toomey Company was $35.20 for inspection fees. This figure is corroborated precisely by the summary of the entire cost of construction for the lighthouse made on May 31, 1911. However, would a penalty fee show up on such a summary? And what about the expense for the days lost due to the delay in delivery?

The answer the Engineer Secretary of the Light-House Board wrote to Toomey & Co. was ". . . the Board finds itself unable to take further action on this claim. You are therefore remitted to the courts for such relief as they may give." In the present study we lack the resources to discover what, if any, satisfaction Toomey & Co. ever received. But for our purposes it really doesn't matter. The issue of how the Board treated the contractor is already very clear. The same theme will come up again when we look at the experience of the keepers who served on the Plum Beach Light.

The design that Major Henry M. Adams provided for the Plum Beach Light was typical of previous models. We have already described at length the similarities between the caisson of Plum Beach and the caisson of the Fourteen Foot Bank designed by Heap. The engineer's plans for the superstructure of the Plum Beach Light correspond exactly with the plans for the superstructure of the Old Orchard Shoal Light in New York—that light to which, in 1892, Third District Inspector Capt. W. S. Schley and Engineer Heap suggested the Plum Beach Light should be similar. In fact this design was used repeatedly. Because of their shape these lighthouses are sometimes called "sparkplug" lighthouses. In Rhode Island the superstructure of the Hog Island Shoal Light of 1901 is very similar to that design. The same thing can be said for Butler's Flat in New Bedford (Massachusetts) Harbor, designed a month or two before the Plum Beach in the fall of 1895. (However, none of these three had a pneumatic caisson foundation.)

Viewing the lighthouse from outside, with the help of the engineering plans, the lowest level that is part of the operation of the lighthouse — just about at the high water mark, or 16 feet below the floor of the large bottom gallery — is the cistern which fills with rainwater.

Next level, the basement, is made up of two parts: (1) an area in the center, the engine room, surrounded by a circular arcade with fancy brickwork and (2) surrounding the arcade, between it and the exterior wall of the building, a series of storage sections, a wood room, a work room, a water closet, an oil storage, two large coal bins, and a large room for provisions. In the center of each level of the lighthouse, running up to the top, were two pipes which ran all the way from the top of the lighthouse through the center of each level, down to the engine room. These pipes contained the weights which operated the clockwork for the light at the very top level and the clockwork for the fog bell in the level just below.

The next level up from the basement included the kitchen and the large covered deck, or gallery. Food would be brought up from the provision room in the basement and prepared and eaten in the kitchen. Next above was the Keeper's Quarters. The level above that, designed to be the Watch Room, became the Assistant Keeper's Quarters. The next level, that of the second gallery, housed the fog bell and the clockwork operating it.

The top level held the light, with a very small third gallery surrounding it.

That is a general description of the interior of the Plum Beach Light, and those who visited when it was cared for found the whole thing very impressive. Adams had followed a good design: he, and other Engineers, probably went to a drawer in the office, pulled out a master plan, of approximately 15 pages, copied it with minor alterations, had the name of the newest lighthouse put at the top, signed the bottom, and dated it. Unfortunately, as described earlier in the chapter, Adams failed to particularize properly an important part, the depth of the caisson.

On May 12, 1899 Engineer Heap sent out a Notice to Mariners. Such a notice was distributed for every change in navigational aids, even for the installation, moving, or removing of a buoy.

NOTICE TO MARINERS.
PLUM BEACH, R.I., LIGHT STATION

Notice is hereby given that, on or about June 15, 1899 a light of the fourth order, flashing white every 5 seconds, will be established in the tower recently erected in the Western Passage, Narragansett Bay, R. I., on the northerly end of Plum Beach Shoal, West side of Channel.

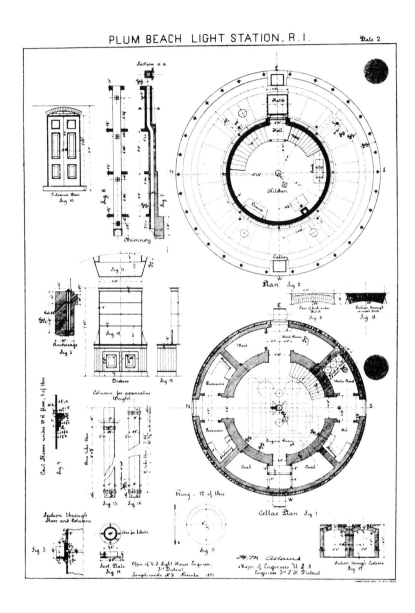

Major Adams' floor plans for the basement and kitchen level replicates standard design.

From microfilm at U.S. Coast Guard Academy Library.

The focal plane of the light will be 53 feet 9 inches above mean high water and the light may be seen 13 nautical miles in clear weather, the observer's eye 15 feet above the water.

At the same time a fog bell, struck by machinery, will be re-established which will strike a double blow every 30 seconds during thick or foggy weather.

The structure consists of a conical iron tower and is painted white below and brown above; the foundation pier is black.

The approximate geographical position of the tower, as taken from the Coast Survey Chart No. 353

Latitude (N) 41 , 31', 49"

Longitude (W) 71 , 24', 20"

The Wickford *Standard* of May 26, 1899 published a slightly different version under the headline "New Light on Plum Beach Shoal," assumed to be the result of a typographical error. The newspaper stated the new light could be seen 128 miles! [In Franklin, New Hampshire?] The paper also departed from official longitude by stating it as 71, 24', 25". ° They added truthfully, "on the same date the temporary red lantern will be discontinued."

We can only hope that bay skippers of that time adhered to the official fixing of the Light's position rather than the erroneous newspaper account. The newspaper's additional five seconds put the position 170 yards *west* of the official locus — which could have put fog-beset vessels smack dab in the middle of the shoal!

The fourth order light rotating so as to flash as indicated in the Notice, put out 1800 candlepower. However, in 1929, because "a stronger light is needed in this locality" approval was given to "increase the candlepower of flashing white light from 1800 to 24,000 by change from 4th order wick lamp to 35 m.m. type A I. O. V. (incandescent oil vapor) lamp."

In order to complete the story of the construction of the Plum Beach Light as it has looked for the last 64 years, we add two more parts:

In the midwinter of 1917-1918 the temperature dropped to record-breaking levels. With the exception of a ferry channel from Saunderstown to Dutch Island the West Passage Saunderstown was frozen solid all the way to Point Judith—so solid people could drive vehicles across. Along the edges of the bay piles of broken ice—six feet high at Plum Beach Point—lined the shore.

Fresnel Lens Fourth Order Lantern from North Light, Block Island.

Courtesy of John Lee.

When the ice began to break up and move down the bay it posed a threat to all the waveswept lighthouses. On February 22, 1918 Charles Ormsby, one of the keepers best loved by Plum Beach people, wrote,

> Inspector:
>
> Referring to Base of light I wish to inform you that the heavy ice this winter has cracked between high and low watermark in one straight line every plate around the base and every plate vertical.
>
> Ormsby
> Keeper

Nancy Blunt Farin, whose family had spent summers at Plum Beach since 1907, remembers Ormsby telling her that in bad weather he could feel the lighthouse sway.

The initial response of District Superintendent J. T. Yates was cool. He claimed that the cracks had been there before, and in reporting that opinion to the Commissioner, said he would investigate further; but the Commissioner's Office wrote him several times asking for a report. Of course, it has to be noted that there was widespread damage to lighthouses up and down the Atlantic seaboard during that winter. The annual report of the Commissioner mentioned a cost of about $400,000.

Comments made by staff members at the Commissioner's office indicate that other cast iron caisson lights, and, in particular other pneumatic caisson lights sustained damage that winter. The technology developed in the 1880's and 90's in hopes of better resisting ice damage had not fared so well as originally hoped in this most severe test. However, Ormsby could have been thankful, if he had known about it, for the persistence of William Ludlow in getting the caisson foundation established deeper into the shoal. Ludlow's concern about adding more riprap had been justified.

At any rate, considering the widespread damage, District Superintendent Yates may have been just too busy to investigate Plum Beach in the spring of 1918.

Finally in July, 1918, he conducted an investigation and sent a report confirming Ormsby's report of February stating, "The crack is open about one inch on the south side of the light and closed on the north side." He also found the vertical cracks, and noted no interior damage from the ice.

And so the placement of an additional 8,000 tons of riprap around the base of the light was put out to bid in 1919, with the explanation that "foundation plates are badly cracked and weakened, and foundation was badly shaken up and weakened by ice. . ." However, because the bids came in so high, the project was dropped for three years.

In February, 1922 Yates proposed going ahead with 9,000 tons of riprap at Plum Beach. A staffer in the Commissioner's office pointed out that less expensive methods of dealing with cracked caissons had been used in other districts, and Commissioner Putnam complained to Yates about the, "considerable expenditure for the protection of one station," and questioned the layout proposed.

Yates replied with a defense of his proposal on February 20,

> This office considers this work necessary at this time and any further delay dangerous, and it is considered that any further delay would not result in any decrease in the cost. The amount of the riprap on the east side has been decreased in order to facilitate the building of boat landing on this side of the structure. The greatest ice pressure at this station is on the north and west sides.

And so the work was ordered and done in that year, 1922; and in 1924 Yates' plan of building a loading dock on the east side of the lighthouse became a reality.

It is fair to say that Charles Ormsby owed a debt of gratitude for his surviving the winter of 1918 as well as he did to the expertise and persistence of Engineer Ludlow. When we think of the survival of the lighthouse and its keepers in the face of the 1938 Hurricane, honor is due not only to Ludlow but also to Ormsby in alerting his superiors to the cracks in the foundation and to Yates for pushing to get the riprap around the lighthouse.

In some respects, D. P Heap contributed more to the Plum Beach Light than Ludlow did. Heap's broad knowledge of innovative technological possibilities had brought the pneumatic caisson type of lighthouse construction into the United States; and that method of construction became available for a place like Plum Beach at a time when no other satisfactory method of construction was available.

Heap was also on the scene as Third District Engineer when important decisions had to be made about approving the idea of building the light, in his reappearance in that position following

Ludlow, in seeing the basic construction project through to its finish, and for taking responsibility for decisions affecting the initial operation of the new light.

But Ludlow was the man to deal with a crisis. During his brief stay in the Third District, he dealt with the engineering crisis of the Plum Beach caisson-depth issue, and with the simultaneous political crisis of negotiating, as middleman, between the the contractor and the Light-House Board the revision of the contract. It was all one crisis, really; and Ludlow had dealt with it with his characteristic intellectual vigor and boldness.

Before we leave Ludlow and his era, there is a part of his career we have not mentioned yet. During his assignment as Military Attaché to the U.S. Embassy in London, Ludlow traveled and studied extensively in northern Europe and the Mediterranean area. He studied the military organizational structures of the European nations, both the internal organization of the military services as well as the way a nation's military services were related to the government and the nation as a whole.

After the Spanish American War, Ludlow reflected, his biographer McAndrews tells us, on the inadequacy of the U. S. military preparation for that war. "Ludlow noted, as had others, the absence of a general staff that could formulate and have ready plans of operations in times of crisis." One of the others was Secretary of War Elihu Root who, in February, 1900, appointed Ludlow President of a Board to produce proposals that would constitute a War College functioning as a General Staff that would oversee and have the power to direct the entire military service. The Board's thorough and comprehensive report, and a separate report Ludlow made during a second trip to Europe, gave Root what he needed to recommend legislation on a War College and a General Staff which Congress passed in 1903. His biographer's comment was that Ludlow "deserves to be better recognized for his seminal input" in the reorganization of the military strength of the United States.

On the way to his next assignment in the Philippine Islands, Ludlow's health, which had been shaky since his illness in Cuba, took a sudden turn for the worse. He died of pulmonary tuberculosis at the age of 57, August 30,1901.

Major General William Ludlow during Spanish American War.

National Archives photo.

There are some surprising similarities between William Ludlow and Nelson W. Aldrich whose influence was so zealously sought in the decision to build the Plum Beach Light!

Of course, there are differences, too. Ludlow was a staunch democrat and Aldrich a staunch and famous republican. Aldrich was more interested in making money than Ludlow — a lot more. Ludlow had a profession in the stricter sense of the word, that involved the educated mastery of a technology while Aldrich's greatest skills were largely self taught.

But both Ludlow and Aldrich, after having fought a variety of battles during their careers, crowned their careers by making a contribution to the nation as a whole, based on an intellectually deep and broad grasp of complex issues each had long dealt with, Aldrich in the area of monetary reform leading to the Federal Reserve System, and Ludlow in the military reorganization just described.

There were some differences in personal style. Ludlow found it easy to get along with people, and did so with warmth; while Aldrich was much more aloof.

But both men had a kind of confidence about their own endeavors and about themselves which was cast in a kind of heroic mold. Aldrich and Ludlow were oustanding examples, but in a broader sense, it was characteristic of the spirit of the era across the nation. It was an era in which the conquest of mainland territory was being finished and succeeded by the conquest of islands; it was an era heady with confidence about harnessing the forces of nature, overcoming technological challenges, and creating industrial and commercial empires.

Mc Cullough, in *The Great Bridge*, quoted earlier in the chapter, sums up the spirit of the age quoting from speeches made at the 1883 dedication of the Brooklyn Bridge: ". . .an astounding exhibition of the power of man to change the face of nature . . .a monument to enterprise, skill, faith, endurance." Later he quotes Lewis Mumford's appraisal of the bridge:

> All that the age had just cause for pride in—its advances in science, its skill in handling iron, its personal heroism in the face of dangerous industrial processes, its willingness to attempt the untried and the impossible—came to a head in Brooklyn Bridge.

The Plum Beach Light was a part of all this although, admittedly, a very small part. Its creation was finally successfully brought about by Miller, an entrepreneur, who was trying to "conquer" Nicaragua, who had a prestigious naval career, and who had conquered a certain portion of the transportation business. Its construction was made possible by the technological brilliance of one engineer, and by the expertise and intrepid personality of another — and, we must not forget, that its success was due also to the exertions of uncounted laborers working under most hazardous conditions.

In later chapters we will see the lighthouse featured in the human struggle against nature. But before that, I'll look at the lighthouse from a completely different point of view.

IV THE LIGHT AND THE LOCAL COMMUNITY

Friendship and Romantic Symbolism

 HUNDREDS OF PEOPLE saw the Plum Beach Light during the first few weeks the completed structure was officially in operation in June, 1899. It was not because any formal or ceremonious attention was granted to this milestone in the history of the lighthouse. (The Light-House Board, like other government agencies of the era, did not have a public relations officer or even a public relations consciousness. The only attention the Wickford *Standard* gave to the event was the official Light-House Board Notice to Mariners, quoted in the last chapter.) The *Standard* gave much more attention to something else that happened at the same time.

The hundreds of people had not come to see the lighthouse. They were passengers on the inaugural and subsequent runs of the newly completed sections of the Sea View Railroad between Narragansett Pier and Wickford. Ultimately this trolley car line would run from Peace Dale to East Greenwich by way of Wakefield, Narragansett Pier, Saunderstown and Wickford. Trolley connections to Providence were available by way of one of the many lines operated by the Union Traction Company of Nelson W. Aldrich and Marsden J. Perry.

That June of '99 the most beautiful 12-mile section of the entire Sea View line had been completed. The ride along the full length of Boston Neck, and then beyond to the Pier, must have been one of the most beautiful land trips available anywhere in Rhode Island. Passengers on the Sea View cars speeding south from Hamilton could look to the southeast, across the marshes and tidal pond Greene's Point, where they got their first glimpse of the new Plum Beach Light resplendent in its fresh coats of brown, white, and black paint.

While traveling along Barber's Heights above Plum Beach, east-looking passengers could trace the Conanicut Island shoreline southward — perhaps, taking quick note of the the new fortifications on Dutch Island and coming to rest on Beavertail Lighthouse and the expanse of the Atlantic Ocean beyond the mouth of the bay.

With all due respect to the "sumptuous banquet" which the Sea View company provided for its guests at the end of the June 17, 1899 inaugural trip at the Metatoxet House in Narragansett Pier, nothing they served could compare with the feast to eye and heart provided by the bay and the ocean for passengers traveling from Plum Beach to Narragansett Pier. A *Providence Sunday Journal* writer was moved to report:

> It was a revelation to some of the guests. . .The ride to Narragansett Pier was thoroughly enjoyed. The road has opened up a country whose beauty is too little known by many of the residents of the State in which it is located. A fine opportunity is given not only to view the country, but also to look out upon the waters of the bay and enjoy the ozone-laden breezes that sweep through the cars in a way that on a warm day is exceedingly refreshing.

The Sea View Railroad and the Plum Beach Light were major enterprises which were both completed in 1899 and which changed the West Passage scene forever. The railroad also changed a large part of South County. (the emotion and attitude-laden name by which Washington County, Rhode Island is called in familiar parlance).

The Sea View did a lot more than bring excursionists to the shore in summer. To begin with, the two daily freight runs carried freight to and from the outlying rural areas on its route. They carried farmers' produce into the villages and cities, and brought perishable foods sent from Providence to more southerly communities. The early morning milk run stopped to pick up the freshly filled 10-quart cans waiting for them on loading platforms along the way.

One of the men on the freight crew was young Edwin S. Babcock, better known as Babbie, who later became a very successful and much loved local businessman and who served as parttime substitute keeper at the Plum Beach Light for about fifteen years. Babbie took the Sea View's freight car all the way into Providence every day, by a special arrangement with the Union Traction Company, owner of the East Greenwich to Providence line.

But the coming of the Sea View had another effect that turned out to be more lasting. It altered the local context in which the young lighthouse and its keepers lived out their days. The passengers on those inaugural runs in June of 1899, and those who followed, liked what they saw. Before the year was out Freeman Tefft responded to the new railroad and to the people's liking what they saw. His farm of about 100 acres, in the family since about 1840, extended from the topmost part of Barber's Heights down to the shore at Plum Beach, and, like thousands of South County farmers after him, he platted most of it. He built a hotel, still standing, right above the trolley line hoping that people would spend a few days, weeks, or the summer at the hotel — then, prizing the land and the beach so much, they would buy property and build.

The idea worked. People liked the hotel. Some families stayed for several summers in a row, and within a few years lots were sold. Scattered amidst the cattle grazing on land not yet sold, the houses went up quickly. Similar results came to Tefft's neighbor to the north, William Edwards, who built a few cottages along the trolley line and up the hill in 1902.

Within one year's time the structure of things in the Barber's Heights summer community changed: In November, 1920 the Sea View, failing in recent years, collapsed permanently. In the summer of 1921 Freeman Tefft died.

In 1922 the Plum Beach Corporation was formed to deal with business concerns of the whole community. In 1924, zealous contemporary accounts tell us, summer residents made a "unanimous choice" to leave behind the name Barber's Heights, so familiar to the early summer colony, and name the whole plat "Plum Beach," a name which, for more than two hundred years, had applied to the stretch of Beach running from north of Plum Beach Point to half a mile south to the Hazard granite quarry, and which had also been associated with the lighthouse and the shoal beneath it. In 1930 the Plum Beach Club was incorporated. In the decades after World War II, and especially after the opening of Interstate route 95 and R. I. route 4, Plum Beach became a year round community combining the spirit of modern suburbia and the old time summer colony.

There is a more complete treatment of the history of the name, *Plum Beach*, in the Appendix. However, it is enough to say that the name stuck more permanently in popular usage to the portion of the beach south of the point near the club's facilities and to the land up the hill, than it did to the lighthouse and to the beach north of the point. Beach plum shrubs still bloom every year south of the point, but the birds and the bugs usually get the fruit before local jelly makers do.

The Plum Beach community was created by the Teffts and Edwardses and others as well as by the people who came and stayed; by the experience of sharing two months together every year; by sharing the unique atmosphere and activities of vacations together; and by the growth of the kind of intimacy and affection which develops in a setting where some of the barriers and defenses of urban life are thrown to the winds. As the old British music hall song went, "You can do a lot of things at the seashore that you can't do in town!" (With appropriate trombones, trumpets, and piano, please!)

The creation of community also depends upon cumulative, shared memories, those associated with unique persons and events which are focused and given substance. At Plum Beach memories were made at the old softball/baseball field, at the tennis courts; in the early days with the hotel and "Old Man Tefft"; and most especially at the beach itself. Long before the club started, a variety of spontaneous zany, and arduous swimming and boating activities took place.

─────────────

One of the most enduring communal focal points was Babbie's store at the corner of Plum Beach Road, and Boston Neck Road. Babbie was a resourceful South County entrepreneur. Like Captain Eaton, he was a realist who knew how to face changes and adapt. Like Eaton he could recognize new opportunities and pursue them with vigor (serving part-time on the Plum Beach Light was one of them). And like the muscular Eaton, he engaged eagerly in a physical challenge. But Babbie also had a social vigor, a way of engaging people which was both intuitive and intellectual. He had the sharpness of mind to organize his family resources into a business that grew and developed into a sixty-four year tradition.

The original shelter for the Barber's Heights trolley stop in front of the hotel had been a retired "California type" trolley car, half open and half closed, parked beside the track. Later a small wooden building was brought from Saunderstown on a flatcar to be used for a shelter. In this building Sam Kelly, operator of a Saunderstown grocery store, ran a store for several summers known as the "Barbers Heights Store." This building later became the first store opened as "Babbie's."

In 1922 Kelly moved the wooden building up to the top of the hill, and Babbie took over. At this corner he could serve the needs of the Barber's Heights customers on the hillside and serve the needs of automobile travelers on the Boston Neck Road. Over the next sixteen years Babbie, his wife, Edith, and their daughter, Helen, developed the store into a multifaceted year round business.

There was something that made Babbie's a gathering place for everyone: summer people, year-round old-time yankees, tourists, navy people, rich and poor, old and young alike. Babbie was known for being blunt, witty, an old skinflint and generous at the same time. When you walked into the store he greeted you with a brisk "yessir!" which was not the least bit obsequious, but rather a challenge for you to state your business and engage in relationship. Babbie looked after people's houses in the winter, occasionally did some real estate work, and was just generally helpful. He was interested in meeting people's needs, and he was definitely interested in making money, but the nature of his transactions were personal, not commercial.

The Babcock's early years had not been easy. They spent one of their first summers camping in a tent. Another summer was spent in an apartment in the Hazard farmhouse. Babbie took on all the work he could get. For several years he was Postmaster in Saunderstown, and they lived over the post office. And in those early years Lighthouse Keeper Ormsby suggested that Babbie serve as part time substitute keeper; two people were always needed on duty, and when there was a day off or a vacation Babbie filled in.

Mr. and Mrs. Babcock were active Lodge members, and rose to statewide offices, he in the Odd Fellows and she in the Rebekahs. In his twenties, still living in Wickford, Babbie had been an active volunteer fireman. In a fire at the Town Hall a piece of falling plate glass severed all the tendons to his right hand and almost took his whole hand. Medical attention and the use of a leather brace enabled him to engage in strenuous activity, even though it was difficult, for the rest of his life.

Keepers and Assistant Keepers of the Plum Beach Light often came to the store to shop, eat, socialize and play cribbage or poker with Babbie. John Ganze, Assistant Keeper during the 30's and Babbie became very good friends and spent a lot of time together, especially in the years before John was married. John helped Babbie with construction of some of his buildings.

For many who were around Plum Beach during the middle six decades of the century, Babbie's was an important communal center

Interior of Babbie's store shows one of 5 tables, bus schedule on post, pay phone left behind counter and Mrs. Babcock presiding assisted by Louise Peters. Johnny Ganze and other keepers over the years stopped in to play cards with Babbie, their substitute keeper.

Courtesy of Bill and Helen Dwelly.

epitomizing the kinds of relationships local people enjoyed and valued. Of course, Babbie had his detractors, too, and people sometimes joked or complained about the "ramshackle" appearance of the old wooden buildings. But when they were torn down to prepare for the opening of the new buildings in 1970, there was weeping among the onlookers, including some of the former complainers.

———————————————

But more significant than any other factor that made for community cohesion was the bay itself. When you came over the brow of the hill, the smell and feel of the salt air would reach and enfold you so that whatever you had been feeling before you got to Plum Beach, you would feel that now you were in an entirely different world. (Of course, on foggy days, that bay atmosphere, too much for a lot of people, would leave the insides of the thin walls dripping and the cottages chilled.)

In the early days, when few had radios, when many had no electricity, the bay was a constant, living symbol of a larger world: as a viable means of transportation beyond the local scene, as a source of powerful weather as a feast for the eyes, as at sunrise or at times when the whitecaps bristled on steel-grey water.

And, as I have explained, because Plum Beach was on a hillside with few trees to obscure the view, the bay was shared by everyone all summer long, and, in an unspoken way, drew people together. In the early decades of the century, the evenings were punctuated by the passing of three Providence to New York boats, two at 8:30 and one at 9:00. Bonfires, Roman candles, or red fire were sometimes lit on the beach to greet the boats which answered with a flash from their search lights or a toot on the whistle. In some households the younger children were sent to bed upon the arrival of the earlier boat, while the older children boasted of staying up until the second boat passed by.

The Plum Beach Light was another explicit, living symbol of community provided by the bay. From 1899 until its closing in 1941 the Light and its keepers were a very important part of what made summer at Plum Beach special. Since I have been a part of this community since my birth, in 1934, into a family with Plum Beach roots back to the turn of the century, this chapter comes to you with an intentional subjectivity that is germane to the subject. Indeed it is at the heart of how and why this book came to be.

The intimate connection between the lighthouse and this neighboring community may be hard to imagine today. While intimacy is highly regarded in other areas of life, the 1980's are characterized by a disjointedness in the fabric of daily routines and public life where there was once a sense of connection and belonging. Local citizens cross local bridges without knowing who turns the lights on, if anyone, or who actually does the maintenance. Customers and staff in some local businesses don't know each others names. And the few lighthouses still working are automated.

But this lighthouse was our lighthouse.

In the second decade of this century the children saw the keepers of the Plum Beach Light as entertaining friends, tour guides and heroes. In Chapter III we met, briefly, Charles Ormsby, one of the best-loved keepers. When he — known to youngsters as "Charlie" or "Lighthouse Charlie" — rowed ashore in the government dory he usually stopped to talk with children and answered their questions about the Lighthouse. One old-timer, the late Roland Siddall, remembered occasions when he would deliver a newspaper to Charlie upon his arrival in the boat.

Charlie made it clear that even though he wasn't allowed to take riders out in his government boat, he would gladly welcome any visitors who came out in their own. The following explanation and narrative about visits to the Plum Beach Light comes from three people who grew up at Plum Beach during the first twenty years of this century: Nancy Blunt Farin, and Florence Kane Foskett, who shared her reminiscences with me during the preparation of this book, and the late Leicester Bradner, who provided an unpublished manuscript he had written when he was Editor of the Barber's Heights *Clamshell,* which he, his brothers, and friends had published when he was a teenager.

Oftentimes children, some as young as ten years old, rowed out by themselves whenever they felt like it. Others made it an annual family excursion. It was a special treat for children to bring guests along. In addition to the Lighthouse trip being a social event, the excitement of the boat ride, the climb from the water all the way to the top, and the tour of the equipment, drew people back again and again.

Rowers approaching the lighthouse brought their boats right up against the cast iron cylinder that was its base. (The substantial pile of

Summer visitors at the Plum Beach Light c. 1915 with keeper (Omsby?) in back. In center seat John Bradner; left of center Lester Bradner, Jr.

Picture by Leicester Bradner.

riprap now seen circling the cylinder and the dock were added, in 1922 and 1924, to the small amount of riprap installed way below the surface of the water when the light was built.) Post cards dating from as early as 1908 illustrated the boarding procedure.

Hearing calls from the visitors in the water about 20 feet below, Charlie, or his assistant, Jim, on the main deck, would let down a rope for them to tie up their boat. Then they would lower the bottom portion of the iron ladder, like a fire escape, and the ascent of the perilous ladder would begin. It was the ambition of every boy in Barber's Heights to scale this ladder, many reputations being made on each trip!

The tour began in the basement, which featured a fresh water cistern and the storage of coal and wood for the stove. The kitchen on the main deck, the Keeper's apartment on the second, and the Assistant Keeper's on the third made a strong impression on visitors: "Immaculate, absolutely immaculate!" Their ascent to each of the upper levels by an iron spiral staircase made visitors feel like characters in a mystery story featuring a murder in an old castle.

For the climax of the tour the visitors stood "in wondering admiration before that highly polished marvel of science, the Great Light. In great solemnity the keeper dissect[ed] and explain[ed] to his awe-stricken audience the intricacies and inmost secrets of the shining monster."

A brief step to the outside of the lantern deck circled by a very slight railing, afforded a lordly view up and down the bay.

In the 1980's, if you walk or drive up the ramp on the western side of the great main span of the 1940 Jamestown Bridge, and pause (pause only if walking) at a point on the ramp due south of the Lighthouse, you will find yourself at the same elevation as the lantern deck of the Lighthouse; looking down the bay you will get almost the same view they had from the lighthouse 75 years ago. Panning from west to east, you'll see the large promontory of the Bonnet, further south and east, the Whale Rock, still holding the stump of the lighthouse destroyed in 1938, the Atlantic Ocean, Beavertail, Dutch Island, the West Ferry dock of Jamestown Village, and, over the top of the lower section of Conanicut, a slight glimpse of Newport on Aquidneck Island.

The last part of the tour of 75 years ago was a visit to the fog bell on the level immediately below the lantern. An explanation of the clockwork that operated the bell, and a demonstration of its loudness was the final treat offered by the revered friendly keeper.

An unpublished article by John Bradner tells of a more dramatic summer visit to the lighthouse:

> . . . two young people paddled Katherine Blunt's canoe out near the lighthouse and there tipped over into the water. This was seen at the beach and immediately two or three fathers grabbed a handy boat to make a rescue. Unfortunately in the excitement, when barely started, they lost an oar and tipped over their boat in the hurry to retrieve the errant oar. Finally everyone was rescued and the lighthouse keeper towed the canoe ashore.

This delightful era came to an end in 1917, when the government, now concerned about World War I, prohibited the visits of civilians to lighthouses. And after the war, the proliferation of automobiles and motor boats provided wider varieties of entertainment.

Traveling by boat was not the only way to reach the Lighthouse, and there were other reasons for going besides visiting the keepers and taking a tour. Over the years adventurous swimmers saw the Plum Beach Light as a goal for a good round trip swim, often done with a companion swimming or rowing alongside. In the early years of the Plum Beach Club, staff members and club leaders, with an eye to their own responsibility and liability, frowned upon club members or their children starting from the club area for freelance escapades of this kind. But, on occasion, the swimming instructor/lifeguard would take upon himself or herself the job of rowing the club skiff to accompany a swimmer deemed qualified for the swim.

Later the "Lighthouse Swim" would become an annual organized event. In recent years the event has been re-routed to the south side of the bridge to the approximate distance of the Lighthouse, sparing swimmers and rowers the challenge of the often choppy water and strong current passing through the spaces between the Jamestown Bridge piers.

The Lighthouse still has some symbolic meaning to people in the community, and sometimes a sketch of the Plum Beach Light appears as a logo on the annual printed calendar of the club. But the change in route for the Lighthouse Swim points out the extent to which the bridge, the location of which years ago caused the closing of the light, and as a spatial and visual barrier, has further eroded the sense of "ownership" people south of the point once had toward the light. For many, detachment has shifted to derision in the 47 years since the closing of the light, owing to its dilapidated condition and erroneous reports of its being for sale for $1.00.

In the years after its closing in 1941, the lighthouse gained in the residential development north of the bridge called Plum Point Shores a new set of neighbors some of whom affectionately claimed "ownership" of the old structure which was so close to them.

However, during the 42 years the light was operating, there were some laughs, some stories about shady happenings, and some high adventure associated with the light that had nothing to do with its mission to aid navigation.

The story has been told, by many who looked out on summer nights during the years of Prohibition, of federal agents pursuing rumrunners in the vicinity of the lighthouse. To this day they remember seeing the lines of the federal agents' tracer bullets. Irving Sheldon, drawing on eyewitness accounts in his *Saunderstown,* reports how that village was a community divided, some in support of the feds, and others in support of the bootleggers. So if the speculation about some lighthouse personnel being involved in rumrunning were true, it would not be a complete surprise, but there is no evidence of it now.

And the reams of archival material on the Plum Beach Light do not tell us whether one keeper's affable demeanor towards visitors was inspired by the bottle as has been alleged. However, one eyewitness claims that, as a teenager in the twenties or early thirties, her church group from the western part of the state was on a picnic near Plum Beach Point and the pastor decided to row out to the lighthouse with her and a few others. When they reached the lighthouse, the informant alleges, and found no one there, they went inside the kitchen where the pastor, she says, found a teapot sitting on top of the unlit stove. He poured alcohol from it and drank.

And the archives provide no evidence to back up the allegations of one old timer about a certain lighthouse staff member regularly visiting a woman in Saunderstown during the daytime while her spouse was at work!

With the exception of the story of the tracer bullets across the water, stories like these could be told, and have been told, about people in all kinds of occupations on land or sea. But these stories are part of the picture of what people on shore thought or felt about the Plum Beach Light and its personnel. The fact that several of the stories have now been told, 50 to 70 years after the events, indicates the strong impact the stories had on my sources even though the passage of time may not have enhanced the veracity of all the details in the telling.

But I have not unearthed any confirmed story of immoral dereliction of duty on the part of Plum Beach Light personnel. However, that was not true of all lights. I take the following story as true because I heard it from a person directly involved, and he could be a very reticent man. John Ganze was Assistant Keeper of the Plum Beach Light during the 1930's. One summer evening he and Keeper Reuben Phillips noticed that the lighthouse at the southern tip of Dutch Island was not lit. Phillips directed Ganze to go down and investigate. By the time Ganze had rowed over a mile down the bay to that lighthouse it was 9:30 pm. He found the two keepers drunk outside the lighthouse. They did not know their light was unlit! They, graciously, invited him to stay over, and, Ganze explained to me, "They were worried I would report them," Ganze told Phillips when he got back to Plum Beach the next day.

When my brother, Steve, age 8, and I, age 5, walked along the beach out to the point in the spring of 1939, we knew nothing of the kind of stories I have just shared. We saw the lighthouse keeper's dory pulled way up and turned over on the dune-like mound that was inshore from the water. We didn't say much, but we were impressed. Perhaps we already knew that our neighbor, Babbie, had been in the Plum Beach Light during the hurricane the previous fall. We didn't say or think we wanted to grow up to be lighthouse keepers, but somehow, Babbie, the boat, and the life it represented were symbolic of what it meant to be a man. And *I* liked to think that we were men already.

It wasn't just the children of the summer colony who respected people like the lighthouse keepers. While there were real differences in style and outlook between the year round "natives" and the summer people from Providence and Philadelphia, many adults of the summer colony respected the knowledge, skill, and strength needed to operate a lighthouse or a ferry boat — something colleges didn't teach. They also knew that their own survival at Plum Beach depended upon the assistance such natives provided for emergencies and the routine management of their property. What the summer people didn't realize was that some natives such as Tefft, Babbie, and Irving Hazard had experience in higher education to match their own.

Of all the impressions the Plum Beach Light made on the people who knew it during the 42 years of its operation certainly the strongest is what they saw and heard from the land and water, by day or night. Everyone who used Plum Beach Road to get to their home saw the lighthouse straight in front of them as soon as they turned down the road.

Nancy Farin treasures memories of the light from her childhood: "When I was little, the lighthouse, with its revolving dome light, flashed in my window and lulled me to sleep every night."

There are some of us who have, if not really good feelings about fog in the bay, at least mixed feelings about the changes which happen with fog. There is a kind of ethereal visual effect, especially when the fog is moving in or departing, that gives an entirely different look to the way familiar landmarks and horizons show up.

Something happens to the way things sound in a fog, too: they sound closer. Today you can sometimes hear, from the top of Barbers Heights hill, the bell buoy north of Dutch Island. For me it is about the best sound left in the bay, aside from the sounds of wind and waves. You can hear the distant sounds from the Breton Reef Tower and Beavertail Lights, but compared with the braying, groaning foghorns of days gone by they sound like quiet woodwinds in an orchestra.

The Plum Beach Light fog signal was part of this maritime symphony. Compared to the great bellowing fog signals from the Beavertail and Point Judith lights on the ocean, the signal from Plum Beach was delicate — a bell that reminded you of high-pitched chimes from a European church tower. Two strokes every 30 seconds. A sound both delicate and firm. Listening closely you could hear some of the mechanism as it was about to strike. And if you were up on the hill during thick fog, it somehow felt as if the lighthouse had transported itself through the fog in your direction. It sounded so close.

Before passing on to you the view of the Plum Beach Light my mother shared with me one night when I was 5, I have to describe what the bay looked like at night from our house, two-thirds of the way up the hill. To be more exact, what the bay didn't look like.

The children of the 1980's, looking up and down the bay and across to the islands at night, see in the foreground a lot of trees and street lights. Beyond that are the bright lights of two major bridges, the Jamestown and the Newport, the glowing orange lights from major highways, the thousands of little lights from suburban developments, a mass of lights from the City of Newport to the southeast, the blue, white, and yellow lights from the airfield and industrial complex at Quonset Point, and, over all this, a glow high in the air, especially above the cities to the north.

All of this may well be considered beautiful; but it wasn't what we saw 50 years ago.

To take in my nighttime world in the spring of 1939 is easy. Start out by blacking out everything described above: none of the recent suburban and industrial developments, no streetlights, no bridges, nothing to speak of at Quonset. Imagine only a few farmhouses visable on the west slope of Conanicut, and, on a clear night, a few lights from Newport, and that's it. Except for one thing.

We were down for the weekend; in those days hardly anyone else arrived as early as May. I had just turned 5, old enough to stay up until dark. My room was on the west side of the house. After I was ready to turn in, my mother asked me to come across the hall and look out my brother's window, on the east side of the house. (She would, a few years later, wake us up one cool August night to come outside and see the Northern Lights. We won't see the Northern Lights again at Plum Beach unless a power blackout coincides with the natural phenomenon.)

That night in 1939 the Plum Beach Light was the only thing I saw as I stood at the window — not the Lighthouse, but the *Light itself.* Even in all that darkness the Light did not look huge, but it was close. Everything was silent in the room, and on the bay, as I watched the thin shaft of light flash to the south and then to the north. Each time the light came around it touched down, a few hundred yards from the lighthouse, on the dark water below.

My time at the window that night was very brief; then I went to bed. But the impression it left with me has persisted for decades. The Lighthouse presented images of sight and sound that conveyed a profound sense of beauty, security, dependability, and peace. And in some way, through the Lighthouse, all of that was there for me.

V   LIGHTHOUSE AND KEEPERS FACE THE ELEMENTS

The 1918 Freeze, Winter Storms, and the Great Hurricane

THE IDEALIZED, romantic view of the lighthouse, which the author and others held over the decades described in the last chapter, is a genuine albeit very personal, part of the history of the Plum Beach Light. But, when we look at the lighthouse through the eyes of the keepers the story takes on a different look.

It is true some of the keepers really liked a keeper's work, and liked being on the Plum Beach Light in particular.

John Ganze, known to his friends as Johnny, liked the assignment at Plum Beach because the land was easily accessible from the light most of the time, unlike the stormy, cold, and lonely assignment at Sakonnet Point Light, where he served before coming to Plum Beach as Assistant Keeper around 1933 or 1934. Johnny enjoyed the sociability he had with some friends on shore, especially Babbie, whom he looked upon as a kind of second father. John's daughter, Alda Kaye, says that he felt the same way about Plum Beach Keeper Reuben Phillips. "He seemed to make friends with men who were fatherly types and who were married to motherly types." He enjoyed having his cherished parrot, given to him by Phillips, with him at the lighthouse, and teaching it words and tricks during the long hours alone at the light.

And Ganze enjoyed being able to do things like getting up on a sunny July morning, saying to Keeper Reuben Phillips, "You make the pancakes; I'll get the blueberries," then rowing over to the Conanicut Island shore where the bushes grew wild in the pastures. Other times he would row over to Plum Beach Point where at low tide a good bed of softshell clams under the stones was there for the digging, good quahogs ready to be scooped out by those who waded offshore or used the tongs from the boat.

And it is also true Edwin Babcock loved working as Substitute Keeper, as his daughter, Helen Dwelly, asserts. An energetic and enthusiastic man, Babbie liked the challenge of rowing out to the lighthouse as well as the responsibility of taking care of the light itself. He enjoyed the peace and solitude he found there most of the time. He liked the view of the bay, and watching the ships go by.

Men who worked on the bay during the era of the Plum Beach Light had a kind of hardiness and endurance that is amazing when seen in the light of the comparative ease of the motorized, electronically sophisticated era of the late twentieth century, in which most of the traffic on the West Passage consists of privately owned pleasure craft. But in the old days there was sometimes a harshness to the elements that went beyond a thrilling challenge. And sometimes there was a loneliness and bitterness that went with being a government employee in an isolated spot. When John Ganze reflected on this side of a keeper's life, he was moved to comment on the rate of suicides among lighthouse keepers.

About hardiness and rowing:

Babbie's son-in-law, Bill Dwelly, describes the kind of challenge Babbie often faced in rowing out to the lighthouse. The current was very strong, the direction depending on the tide. If faced with a combination of an outgoing tide and a northeast wind, it was very hard to reach the Lighthouse dock on the east side of the structure from Plum Beach. The strategy was to row against the wind to a point far north of the light, make a turn, come by the dock, catch the rope hanging down from the dock, attach it to the cleat and, after pulling in close to the dock, climb the ladder up the side, and then winch the boat up for storage on the dock.

Following this strategy on a day of strong northeast wind Babbie rowed up far to the north, made the turn, and was pushed along so quickly that he shot right by the dock, and on missing the rope, was dragged by the wind and current all the way down to Casey's Point, about a mile to the southwest, before he could get the boat turned around to try again.

While such rowing activity was apparently accepted, and expected as a part of life during the nineteenth and early twentieth centuries there were, even in the old days, limits to what was considered reasonable risk taking. And so the Wickford *Standard* on

July 15, 1898 took note of the exceptional rowing of a Captain Clark during the previous week: an amazing twenty-mile-long trip to Pawtuxet, at such an advanced age ("considerably over sixty")!

"Lighthouse Charlie" Ormsby, who had affably entertained summer colony guests on the light fifteen years before, faced a life-threatening challenge that was reported in the *Sunday Journal* of January 29, 1928.

> Ormsby. . .was capsized when the rough waters whipped up by a strong wind filled his boat with water late yesterday afternoon as he was voyaging ashore. Although Ormsby managed to make shore, he had to leave the boat and was unable to return to the light.

Of course there is something wrong either in the accuracy of the news report or in Ormsby's leaving the lighthouse untended in the late afternoon during the winter. Captain Eaton called the Coast Guard because of the urgent need to get someone on the lighthouse to get the light going for that night; the Coast Guard notified the lighthouse tender *Pansy* which came around the north end of Conanicut from Newport, and made several efforts to steam down to the lighthouse and drop off a man to start and tend the light in Ormsby's absence. The driving snow was so bad, they couldn't do it. They returned to Newport, leaving the Plum Beach Light dark for one night.

During the winters of 1917-18 and 1933-34 the Narragansett Bay froze over, solid. It has been said that during 1917-18 the ice was so thick people drove horsedrawn wagons on it, and that during 1933-34 people drove automobiles across. But the winter of 1918 was a milestone for the Plum Beach Light. During that year the ice extended beyond the bay down to Point Judith. The ferry was able to keep a path open through the ice between Saunderstown and Dutch Island, and that was a help to the military personnel stationed there; but Dutch Island was as far as the ferry got.

Lighthouse historian, Richard Champlin, cites the report that the structure was actually "tilted" during that great 1917-18 freeeze, and later righted. It is hard to believe this story. Champlin received the information by way of Captain Archie Arnold from Archie's uncle, Horace Arnold, Keeper at different times of the Conanicut Point Light and the Conimicut Point Light. There is no mention of a "tilt" in the voluminous correspondence between the Plum Beach Keeper, the District Superintendent, and the Commissioner in Washington, about the winter's damage at Plum Beach and the means of dealing with it.

John Bradner and others who visited Plum Beach Point in January of 1918 saw, running across the rough surface of the thick ice in the direction of the lighthouse a trail that looked like marks made by the keel of a boat being dragged. The keepers probably had to pull it most of the way, but they had to have the boat in case there was a break in the ice during their transit.

We have no further reports of any kind now available about what happened to the Plum Beach Light and its keepers that winter. However we can piece together some idea of what it was like.

Earl Caswell, another one of Richard Champlin's informants, told me the same story he told Champlin seventeen years before: the keeper of the Whale Rock Light, Captain Tooker, was stranded, his boat stuck in the ice between the light and the shore for eight hours, until rescuers on shore could find a way to tow him to shore across the ice. Ormsby had a longer row than they did at Whale Rock. We can only guess what it might have been like for him, especially before the ice was completely solidified and after it had started to break up.

When the ice did begin to break up, it came pushing down the bay. Much further north at the Conimicut Point Light, where the wind did not have such an expanse of bay in which to build up momentum as it did in the West Passage, Horace Arnold was keeper. Richard Champlin learned from Captain Archie Arnold that Horace reported the ice crashing against the Conimicut Point Light with such vigor that he expected it would be destroyed, and feared for his life. His colleague had the boat ashore, so Arnold resorted to extraordinary measures. He threw his mattress onto an ice floe, jumped onto it, and went floating down the bay at a great clip, until he was picked up by the astounded captain of the tug *Gaspee.*

At Plum Beach, remember, the only riprap around the lighthouse at that time was far below the surface of the water. The huge pieces of thick ice pounded against the cast iron shell of the foundation as it came down the bay driven by the pressure of severe wind and the tide. The damage to the caisson of the Plum Beach Light was just a part of the $400,000 worth of damage the freeze of 1917-18 did to lighthouses of the Atlantic Seaboard. Considering the extreme effects which the ice had upon the waveswept lighthouses of the bay, it is not surprising someone would exaggerate a detail of the story fifty years later at the time Champlin was doing research for his 1971 articles.

(John Ganze in 1933-34, his first winter at Plum Beach, saw the ice piling up on the rocks around the lighthouse as high as the portholes in the basement. And sometimes the ice moved the rocks. "You could hear it crunching. It was scary," he said.)

The story of the 1917-18 Freeze is one of two stories about the lighthouse oldtimers of Plum Beach are likely to tell their children, grandchildren or visitors. The other story always takes priority. It is the story of the 1938 Hurricane.

About 2:30 on the afternoon of September 21, 1938, Babbie released the rope which tied the dory to the dock on the east side of the lighthouse, and started to row for shore. He did not know a hurricane was on the way, but it had already started to rough up Long Island in a bad way. Trees on that island were going down under winds estimated at 90 miles an hour. Boatmen were already in serious danger, and people were desperately planning to abandon vulnerable beach homes.

Babbie was eager to get to shore. As Substitute Keeper he was replacing Keeper Reuben Phillips who was visiting his family in Vermont. Babbie had been on the lighthouse for three days now, alone when Assistant Keeper Johnny Ganze had a day off. It had been raining steady for four days. Now it was his turn to get some time off, to get back up to his home and business to rejoin his wife and his 22-year-old daughter, Helen. They were as usual, carrying on their gasoline, restaurant, grocery, and tourist cabin business in his absence.

Babbie was known for being a strong willed individualist. He was sometimes downright stubborn. When someone built a house across an established right-of-way to the shore, he made a habit of getting a key to it and walking through the house at least once a year to maintain the status of the right-of-way. His daughter, Helen, later said of him, "My father was always right, whether he was wrong or not!"

Once, in later years, when the gasoline distributor called, as they often did, to announce a change in the pump price of the fuel he and other dealers had on hand from 24.9 cents down to 22.9, cents he put the phone down and told his son-in-law, Bill Dwelly, "They're not going to make me change it." Bill loved his father-in-law but nevertheless referred to him as an "old skinflint." He tried to argue Babbie around to changing the price of the gas by pointing to business he might lose to competitors who lowered the price. "It's my gas," Babbie said, " and I'll charge what I want for it."

Babbie wasn't a man easily put off from something he aimed to do. But when he found himself contending with the heavy waves and wind that were now chopping up the bay, he realized that he had met his match. With some difficulty he turned the boat around and returned to the Lighthouse.

Johnny had been watching from the Light, and as soon as the dory reappeared at the dock he was ready to take charge. He knew what to do when a storm was brewing.

John Ganze was twenty nine, seventeen years younger than Babbie, but was more experienced in lighthouse work. He started at Highland Light in New Jersey at age seventeen, after lying about his age, and in 1930 went to Sakonnet Point Light, where rough ocean storms were common. John had hated Sakonnet Point. Even though Johnny looked on Babbie as a father, he took pride in having greater expertise than Babbie, the part-time substitute.

Ganze took charge of lifting up the dory on to the dock and lashing it with Babbie's help to the wrought iron stanchions of the railing on top of the dock. They glanced down the bay and noticed the ferry, *Hammonton*, under Captain Archie Arnold, which had set out from Jamestown at 3:00 PM on its regular trip to Saunderstown. While the ferry struggled with the stormy seas, the two keepers at the Plum Beach Light stored things they could easily carry and tied down what they couldn't. Within half an hour the wind had gotten so rough and the waves so menacing, they had to go inside and secure the portholes, windows, and doors in the basement and the main deck.

Leicester Clark, Quartermaster on the *Hammonton*, was trying to bring the ferry around the north end of Dutch Island and across the main channel of the West Passage toward Saunderstown. Before he got as far as the bell buoy north of Dutch Island, he turned to Archie Arnold and said, "Cap, she's not answering the helm!" Arnold could see how bad things looked. "Okay," he answered, "Let's bring her around, and we'll head back to Jamestown."

By the time Clark had brought the *Hammonton* around to head back, Babbie and Johnny, now securely shut up inside the lighthouse, could no longer see her, for the storm had become so thick.

At the time Babbie had been rowing back to the Lighthouse, Helen, his daughter, was sitting with a friend in the movie theater in East Greenwich waiting, with a lot of other people, for the electricity to come back on so they could watch the double feature they had driven to see. The movies advertised were *Bride for Henry*, and *I Am The Law* with Edward G. Robinson. They never saw the movies. After half an hour's wait the management announced that they had the choice of either taking a "raincheck" for another day, or waiting for the resumption of electrical power that afternoon. Helen and her friend elected to take the raincheck, and left.

While Helen was waiting for the movie and Johnny and Babbie were locking themselves up inside the Plum Beach Light, another drama was being played out about a mile south of the lighthouse in the middle of the West Passage. It is a story worth telling in its own right, but we share it here because it contains the only news about the Plum Beach Light and the Hurricane ever to get into print beyond the local area until the Champlin articles of 1971.

Scott Chapin, from Saunderstown whose family owned the 40-foot steel-hulled "whaleback" sloop *Moby Dick,* moored at the Saunderstown Yacht Club, was at the club that afternoon with his friend, Richmond Crolius from South Kingstown. Scott decided to secure the *Moby Dick* with another line to its mooring against the storm that was upon them. They launched a skiff with great difficulty and rowed out to where the sloop was moored. As Crolius described the situation later in the Delta Phi *Record,* " I was on the nose, just making fast the inboard end of the warp, when Scott's head appeared in the cockpit astern. About that time a comber caught her and sent the bow up with a rush. The line [to the mooring] snapped and then the fun started."

Scott managed to get the engine started in time to prevent them from crashing into rocks on the Saunderstown shore, and Richmond, in a precarious position on the streamlined bow, made his way back to the cockpit and began attaching an anchor to the end of the line he had attached at the bow.

Since the wind was coming from a southeasterly direction, the plan was to head for protection of a lee shore, and Dutch Island, three-quarters of a mile to the east, was their best hope. The narrow passage between Saunderstown and Dutch Island often has a rough current. On the afternoon of September 21, 1938, the crossing was impossible; in the fully risen sea. Crolius noticed that up to five feet above the water a thick spume blew at them ahead of the waves. Others have described this phenomenon as the wind lifting large "sheets" of water off the waves and blowing them through the air. They never got to Dutch Island, and instead passed back and forth in a north-south circuit in the channel between Saunderstown and Dutch Island, going as far south as the Dutch Island Light.

Then the motor gave out.

With hindsight it would be easy to criticize the decision to go out to the *Moby Dick* at all on that afternoon. Even when they pushed off from shore in the skiff things looked hazardous, with the wind blowing about 45 miles per hour. But they didn't know that this was a

Hurricane, nor that the chances for safety for anyone on the water were rapidly deteriorating.

They were young men of college age, experienced sailors who well knew the bay. Remarkably, they kept cool heads in a life-threatening crisis and handled the storm as best they could. They decided to ride up the bay with the storm, using their thick mast as the only "sail".

At the Plum Beach Light the waves were pounding ten feet above the riprap onto the gallery deck where the two keepers were barricaded in the kitchen. Ganze and Babbie then headed for the iron spiral staircase, carrying the portable radio, Babbie's flask of whisky, and some water. They sought refuge just above the kitchen in the Keeper's quarters which Babbie was using in the absence of Keeper Phillips.

The fury of the storm increased as the waves smashed higher against the lighthouse. Babbie, always vocal and sometimes a vociferous man, openly expressed his fear. Ganze, a reserved person, kept insisting, quietly, that he had gone through worse storms at the Sakonnet Point Light. But Babbie knew the West Passage and its weather better than Ganze, and sensed that the weather they now faced was far different from storms of the past. Babbie had reason to be afraid. By this time the storm was destroying homes and lives on the south shore of the state from Watch Hill to Point Judith. At the lighthouse the waves were breaking freely around the kitchen, and pounding hard against the doors.

Babbie looked out the east window of the quarters. He saw, as reported in the September 24 Providence *Journal* "a streamlined yacht going by at 60 miles per hour." Apparently Babbie recognized the *Moby Dick* and later gave the names of the occupants, assuming they could not have survived. Scott Chapin and Rich Crolius were reported dead.

What actually happened to Crolius and Chapin was that as the sloop sped up the bay, they held to the eastern side of the West Passage. Before passing north of the end of Conanicut, wanting to avoid the danger of the wide open expanse of bay to the northeast, they decided to try to steer the *Moby Dick* around to the north and west of Fox Island and look for a place to land on the mainland. They succeeded and rode into the midst of some partially submerged pines at Anthony's Beach north of Bissell's Cove and finally came to rest 200 yards inland from the shoreline.

The young survivors secured the *Moby Dick* to some of the pines among which they had ended their unexpected ride up the bay, then

Maurice Chapin's sloop "Moby Dick", driven ashore by the 1938 hurricane after passing the Plum Beach Lighthouse.

made their way through pastures covered with "choppy brackish water" to Hamilton. There, the two sailors got a ride, weaving their way around fallen trees to Saunderstown where they found that their belongings and the Crolius family car had been destroyed along with the Yacht Club. They also found a couple of stiff drinks of rum with friends.

At the lighthouse Ganze and Babbie shared Babbie's whisky that afternoon making use of the water they had carried up from the kitchen as a mixer.

(Considering all the death and destruction that took place in Rhode Island and nearby states that day, it is not surprising that the only item getting into print concerning the Plum Beach Light was the story of the sighting of the *Moby Dick* and a brief report in the *R.I. Pendulum* of East Greenwich. In contrast to many other reports that reached newspapers, the full story of the Plum Beach Light did not appear as dramatic at first glance. No one pursued it further until Richard Champlin's 1971 article.)

The storm was such that it isolated individuals and small groups in the horror of their own crises. All over the state people were making their unique responses to their own crises. Only a very few people had an idea of what was happening elsewhere.

The storm was now so thick Babbie and Johnny were not aware of what happened to the *Hammonton,* which they had last seen shortly after 3:00. In ordinary weather the keepers could have seen the Jamestown West Ferry slip. The *Hammonton,* arriving back at 3:30 after the aborted attempt to cross to Saunderstown, could not actually pull all the way in to the slip to hook up to the dock's apron. Because of the heavy seas and flooding of the dock a safe landing simply could not be made. The eighteen passengers expressed a preference not to risk trying to disembark under the circumstances. Keeping the engine going at slow to half speed ahead Captain Arnold kept the ferry inside the protection of the slip pilings. By 4:00 P.M. he found time to write in the log that the ferry was secured "with all available lines. . .Dock flooded, impossible to go ashore." The *Hammonton* was riding so high that Arnold wrote "Vessel's guards over pilings on North side of slip. .."

Neither the two keepers nor those on the *Hammonton* knew what was then happening nearby on the road across that narrow strip of beach that connects Beaverhead with the rest of Conanicut. It was a struggle which would sear the hearts of survivors and families concerned for decades to come. A small Jamestown school bus carrying eight children was overwhelmed and swept off the road by huge waves. The driver tried to get them all away from the swamped bus to safety. But only he and one boy survived. The boy was Clayton Chellis, son of Carl Chellis, Keeper of the Beavertail Light. Clayton's sister, Marion, was one of the children who died next to the bus.

Ganze and Babbie would find out later about the death of the keeper's wife and son and three others at the Sand Point Light on Prudence, about the injury suffered by the keeper, Robert Gustavus, who was for a time washed out into the bay, and about damage to buildings at light stations throughout the state. And they would find out later what had happened at Whale Rock.

Plum Beach Light was now having its own adventure. The constant flow of the water going up the bay was now at the level of the kitchen 15 feet above the usual high tide. The waves, pounding twenty feet up onto the windows of the Keepers Quarters sent the two men up the iron spiral staircase to the next higher level. They were now on the fourth level, Johnny Ganze's Assistant Keeper's Quarters. Babbie, with openly expressed horror saw shacks, boats, and houses, going by on either side of the lighthouse, and felt the whole building tremble with the onslaught of wind and wave.

John Ganze resisted fear. This quiet and reserved man, who spent hours studying the complicated subject of civil service law and the stock market, had his own dramatic way of reaching beyond his inner world. He loved adventurous risk-taking; he loved danger. He gambled at poker with Babbie sometimes, and played the stock market. But taking life-threatening risks was important to him. An old photo shows him standing, without support, on the edge of the railing foundation that circles the main deck gallery of the lighthouse—a twelve foot drop to the rocks on one side. When the Jamestown Bridge was later being built next to the lighthouse, he would walk out along the bridge after the construction crews had left for the day and climb up onto the steel superstructure above the main span—150 feet above the water.

So it went against the grain for John Ganze to acknowledge fear in the face of physical danger. But before the afternoon was over he would know fear. His explanation of it decades later was that Babbie's getting so scared was what made him scared.

There was also a contrast in how people dealt with the storm emotionally in the family quarters behind Babbie's store. Helen Babcock had gotten home from the Greenwich Theatre at about four o'clock after a very difficult ten mile ride with sand blowing against the windshield and trees and wires falling in front of her. She considered cutting the trip short and stopping at the police station in

Wickford. But she was in such a hurry to get inside her own home that, after dropping her friend off, she drove straight into the garage in one sweeping turn from Plum Beach Road. "Didn't hit a thing! That's the one and only time I ever made that garage without backing up," Helen said later.

Helen and her mother sat with others who had been in the store at the time, looking out the windows on the east side of the family quarters. With all the wind, sand, salt spray and rain coming at them, they couldn't see the bay a third of a mile down the hill. Edith and Helen, in rocking chairs, were laughing. The wind had a rhythmic force about it, and the whole panel of window frames would repeatedly buckle in toward them and then snap outward. As the two of them rocked in their chairs, they chanted and laughed together, over and over again, "Here she comes! . . There she goes!. . . " They just sat there and roared, making a joke out of the whole thing. The others with them in the room didn't like the way the two Babcock women were reacting to the storm and told them so.

At the lighthouse things were bad. The continued onslaught of wind and now 30-foot waves broke open the kitchen door and the portholes in the basement below. As the water rushed through, Babbie and John saw their ice box, containing a cooked chicken, a pound of butter, some eggs and bacon, washed right out of the building and on up the bay. The coal stove was pushed to the side of the room. The water swept through windows in the Keeper's quarters and washed clear through the bedroom. Then, one of the most alarming sights of the storm: they saw their boats go up the bay.

As the raging water crashed inside the building below them and against the building above them, Babbie and John headed up to the fog bell room. This was as high as they could go; it would be too dangerous on the lantern deck above them. As they stood there Ganze felt the whole building vibrate under the pressure of wind and water.

This Assistant Keeper and this Substitute Keeper were an ideal team, not only because they were good friends, but because of their differences. Babbie's fear had made him turn back to the lighthouse, and his open expression of his fear had alerted his stoic young colleague, who didn't want to admit fear, to the need for action. While Babbie's fear was close to panic, John was the one who knew what to do and formulated their plan of action. However, Johnny acknowledged later, "If I'd been alone, I'd a gone crazy."

Now Johnny Ganze was afraid, and he knew it.

Ganze was worried about the light itself. With the lens apparatus and the rotating device it was very heavy. If it fell, he feared the damage to the structure, and perhaps to them, would be great. Of particular concern was the mercury. The base of the huge lantern contained a thick film of mercury upon which the lantern, when lit, constantly revolved. Ganze was worried that the vibrations, caused by the violent storm, would upset the lantern, its base, and some extra flasks of mercury nearby. If the mercury fell on them it would be lost to further use. Even worse, it could cause even more injury to the keepers.

Johnny pulled shut the iron trap door separating them from the light chamber above and then bolted it.

There was only one other thing they could do. They had climbed as high above the raging flood as they could. The water they had brought up from the kitchen was now gone. They had stopped drinking Babbie's whisky because they didn't want to drink it straight and get drunk in the midst of all the danger.

They took rope and lashed themselves, back to back, against the pipe containing the clockwork weights that ran from the chamber above down to the basement. If the lighthouse went over, as they feared it would, they would at least be found together.

If you talk to people who were on the bay, on the south shore, or in downtown Providence on that late afternoon of September 21, you will get conflicting views as to whether or not there had been a *tidal wave* in that storm. The same applies if you read contemporary accounts of the storm. Perhaps it is a matter of semantics or where the witness was during the storm. Everett S. Allen's stirring, well researched book, *A Wind to Shake the World*, which attempts to cover the storm in southern New England and southern New York, tells us time and again of people in different coastal locations reporting, in the late afternoon, a wave higher than all the rest. Some reported it at 40 feet, some 60, and one even reported it to be 100 feet in height.

Within a month after the storm the Providence *Journal* published its comprehensive classic, *The Great Hurricane.* (It was printed in the brown rotogravure customary in those years, and it became a favorite book in Rhode Island homes during many decades after the storm.) The book provides a lengthy and complex meteorological explanation of the storm and the "tidal wave." On September 21, 1938 normal high tide was scheduled for Providence at 6:52. That fact coupled with extreme tidal conditions associated with the autumnal equinox (its height any and all years on September 21) PLUS hurricane winds blowing up the bay from the southeast and later the southwest at 120 miles per hour and gusting higher combined to make this the worst storm in Rhode Island since the Great Gale of September 22(!) 1815.

In the late afternoon as the eye of the circular storm passed up the Connecticut Valley to the west, and the direction of the winds hitting Rhode Island began to shift from southeast to southwest combining for a while with the northerly direction of the whole storm just at the time the equinoctial tide was reaching its peak, a tremendous force drove a rogue wave up the narrow passages of the bay, being oriented in the same northerly direction as the storm.

Ganze and Babbie, tied to the pipe, waited for what seemed to be inevitable disaster. As the height of the water rose higher than at any time all afternoon and the wind drove harder, a sudden force shook the whole structure. To John Ganze it seemed as if a giant broom had taken a swat at the lighthouse. As the wind and waves continued to crash against the upper levels of the building, they sensed a strange kind of pressure, which they later described as a "vacuum," being created within the structure.They could feel it in their ears. They feared the lighthouse would crumble. They untied themselves and opened portholes to relieve the pressure.

While the two men were thus occupied, the concrete walls on the inside of the iron cylinder of the building were, as Johnny later described it, cracking "like an eggshell." And cracks discovered after the Freeze in 1918 in the external cast iron plates of the caisson were opening wider. New cracks in the cast iron were also developing.

Babbie and John returned to the bell chamber and waited, this time without lashing themselves. There were no more swats from the giant broom, but the building continued to shake against the raging storm. John Ganze, years later, acknowledged, that "if it had gone on ten minutes longer we'd a been gone!"

(At the height of the storm in Providence Plum Beach summer resident, Nathan M. Wright, Jr.,.and his staff at 85 Westminster Street looked out from second-story windows in horror at the flood washing over the roofs of long stalled trolley cars. The wind was actually lifting roofs, chimneys and awning frames of other buildings and smashing them against or near their building. They watched a man hanging half naked from a barber's sign across the street, but were helpless to save him from drowning.)

(About a mile to the east of Westminster Street the tug *Gaspee*, which had rescued keeper Horace Arnold from the ice floe twenty years before, was losing a battle with the hurricane in the Seekonk River. When it smashed against the railroad bridge, the crew escaped in a dory, but gallant to the end, they stopped to rescure a girl holding on to wreckage in the midst of the flood.)

Sometime around 7:00 P.M. the force of the storm and the intensity of both wind and waves began gradually to die down. At Plum Beach as the overfull bay began very slowly to recede to its normal level, the two keepers started, level by level, to see what was left of their drenched, battered station.

Plum Beach Light had just had tons of water forced through it, and what had been for these keepers a place of comfort and security, austere as it may have been, was now strewn with the wreckage of the hurricane. It was a mess.

At the top of the lighthouse, two of the half-inch bolts that secured the base of the great lantern to the 1-1/4 inch iron floor had been loosened.

In the Assistant Keeper's Quarters, John Ganze's belongings were washed away or ruined. Looking among the wreckage in the kitchen and the basement they found that the food that hadn't sailed up the bay in the ice box was ruined. Fresh water had been tainted by dirty salt water and was leaking out through cracks in the cistern. Outside the forged steel poles of the dock railing, to which they had so carefully lashed the dory, were bent over like wet spaghetti hanging from a fork. Both of the boats were gone.

The darkness of the storm had already merged into the darkness of the evening, and the waters were receding faster now. (Babbie and Ganze would not get a full picture of the damage until the next morning.) Yet they could see that huge pieces of debris were banging against the riprap and not against the lighthouse itself. Some of the pieces, perhaps parts of houses, docks, and boats, were lodged in the rocks.

Later in the evening when the air had cleared, they looked out to the south, they saw no light burning at Whale Rock and wondered aloud what that could mean.

By eleven that night the waters at the Jamestown's West Ferry had receded to the normal level, leaving a broken-up dock and the *Hammonton* "heeled down to a 30° port list" because the guard rim of the starboard side had caught up on top of the north pilings of the slip. Earlier efforts to move the ferry out of the slip to prevent that awkward situation had failed because the ship was already caught on the pilings. And so at 11P.M., the log reports, the 18 passengers, the crew, and captain were finally able to disembark, not in the normal way, but by ladder and planks. The eight vehicles stayed on the ferry until it arrived the next day at the Newport dock which was still intact.

Half way up the hill above Plum Beach Cynthia Gowdy, Nathan Wright's mother-in-law and her husband Mahlon, both in their seventies prepared for bed in their summer home which had rocked on its concrete post foundations for several hours that afternoon. She wrote in her diary "How can I ever record the terrible Hurricane that has lashed R. I. today. Terrible destruction to life and property. I never was so frightened."

When Helen Babcock looked out the east window on the morning of September 22 she saw one of those fall days that ordinarily makes a person feel good about living by the bay: clear blue sky, bright sun, and a northeast wind driving whitecaps down the dark blue bay. On such a day she could have enjoyed watching the waves break onto the riprap on the north side of the Plum Beach Light, and the tide-rip effect south of the lighthouse where the onrush of water, split by the bulk of lighthouse and riprap, would splash back together again.

But not today. Helen held a spyglass to her eye and didn't like what she saw: Most of the railing on the main gallery of the lighthouse was missing, parts of the gallery roof were gone, and some of the steel stanchions were bent over. Then she saw a flag hanging upside down.

During the storm she had no way of knowing what was going on out on the bay, what with so much going on around them on land and the poor visibility. The dock on which the keepers' boats were kept was on the east side of the lighthouse and not visible from the hill. She didn't realize that the boats were gone. Now she remembered, from Girl Scout training that an upside flag down was a signal of distress. What could have happened on the lighthouse? What could she and her mother do now?

How the two keepers got through the night we will never know. On any night one of the keepers is expected to keep alert and watching for trouble. How or where could either of them have slept given the condition of the place and given what they had been through?

In the morning John Ganze looked out to the south from the top of the lighthouse. He scanned the lower bay and the ocean now

View from the north shows damage and debris at the Plum Beach Light after 1938 hurricane.

Picture courtesy of U.S. Coast Guard historian.

dazzling in the sunlight. He turned abruptly and hurried below shouting "The Whale Rock is gone!"

He joined Babbie at a broken window. They both looked out in horror. The violence which had torn up the sea wall at Narragansett Pier and the new one at Point Judith, which had demolished the ferry slip at Saunderstown, and had swept away the clubhouse at Plum Beach, had broken the Whale Rock Light from the top of the concrete-filled caisson. All they could see was the stump of the foundation of that once staunch lighthouse.

They knew that at least one of their colleagues had been in the light when it went. It was a fate they had narrowly escaped themselves.

Later they would learn that Keeper Daniel Sullivan had been ashore getting groceries when the storm struck and was spared. Assistant Walter Eberle, who had a wife and six children, was in the light. His body and the broken structure of the light itself, were never found.

There are three possible explanations as to why the Whale Rock Light went down in the storm and Plum Beach Light didn't. First, Eberle may not have had the presence of mind to open windows and relieve some of the pressure, as John and Babbie had. It is reasonable to assume that a person alone, under the circumstances, could panic at a time when practical measures are called for.

Secondly, being right at the mouth of the bay, the Whale Rock Light received a stronger blast from the storm coming across the ocean. This was John Ganze's view. Others held that the narrow passage of the bay funneled the storm with greater force onto the lighthouses in the West Passage, and farther north. The Sakonnet Point Light, which was of similar construction to Whale Rock and even more exposed to the ocean than the Whale Rock, survived with damages similar to the Plum Beach Light.

Thirdly, there is Richard Champlin's provocative contention about some known defect in the structure of the Whale Rock Light at a level just above the foundation, a weakness which the storm exploited. This idea deserves the extensive study necessary to resolve it.

Whatever the causes, the destruction of the Whale Rock Light strongly affected Babbie and Ganze on the Plum Beach Light.

In the full light of day Ganze and Babcock assessed their situation and the condition of the lighthouse. They found the cracks

Before: Old postcard of Whale Rock Light.

Courtesy of Sarah Gleanan.

After: Foundation of Whale Rock Light after the 1938 hurricane.

Picture by Wilfred. E. Warren.

on the inside walls of the basement. The cast iron caisson had taken a beating: the cracks discovered in 1918 were reopened, some of the seams were opened, and new cracks had formed.

Many of the iron footplates around the main gallery were destroyed, and about a third of the concrete deck of the gallery was ripped up, in some instances exposing the brick arches of the basement ceiling below. The storm had torn, ripped and bent the railing, stanchions, and roof of the main gallery and sent a large section of the railing into the water where it stood resting on the underwater portion of the riprap. The only thing on the gallery that had survived were the quahogging tongs secured in the crevice where the gallery roof met the cast iron wall of the building. There was considerable shifting of the riprap rocks, some of which weighed 4 tons, and some had been knocked off the upper levels of the pile.

Out on the large concrete dock, which had been built right up against the iron caisson in 1924, walking by the broken and bent railing which they had noticed last night, the two men now discovered how extensive the damage to the dock was. The entire pier, which weighed about 130 tons, had been pulled away from the caisson by about a foot. The wooden cantilever-type extension off the end of the dock was wrecked.

And then, amidst the storm debris that approached the lighthouse as the flood receded, their own ice box came banging up against the riprap. Johnny Ganze grabbed a boat hook and pulled it in. He later told of opening it up: the cooked chicken was still there, but the pound of butter gone. Who would want to take something like that? But now no one would want the chicken either.

The grim fact was they had no boat, no food, and no water. The storm-ravaged lighthouse was vulnerable. There was no way to communicate with the shore (aside from the upside-down flag which Babbie put up), and no one was coming to get them. Ganze said later that this experience would stay with him the rest of his life.

The more Helen thought about her father and Johnny Ganze on the lighthouse the more she felt she had to do something. Along the Plum Beach shore, there were no boats. All boats that had not been locked up in barns by departing summer people were now stove in on rocks or swept away. Not long after she had made her way home the day before, more trees had fallen on the way to Wickford, and now no one could drive through. Since their phone was still working, Helen decided to call the police. She described the damage to the lighthouse and their signal of the upside-down flag. She got a promise of help, but it never came.

John O. Ganze and Edwin S. Babcock watched and waited. It appeared that no one was concerned about them, and they couldn't understand why. A Coast Guard cutter went by with dignitaries on board surveying damage around the bay. The people on deck waved pleasantly. The two keepers waved wildly, but the cutter kept going. It went by again later in the day and again did not stop. A few Army planes went over that afternoon. But no one came to help them.

At 4:09 that afternoon the office of the Lighthouse Commissioner in Washington received a telegram from The Second Lighthouse District Superintendent, George Eaton, with his assessment of the damages sustained in his district. Plum Beach and others with similar damage were not mentioned.

Twenty-four hours had passed since the storm had driven the keepers into the upper reaches of the Plum Beach Light. They had not eaten for more than a day and had not had a drink since they had used the last good drinking water with Babbie's whisky during the storm.

The two men were extremely upset. Babbie was not only worried, but angry. It was bad enough that the government had failed to come to their assistance, but where was his family? John had been married for only a few months, and his young wife lived farther away in Saunderstown, but Babbie's family was just up the hill. They were a close family. Why didn't they come, or send someone? But, on the lighthouse they didn't know about the widespread devastation nor about the disappearance of boats on the shore.

The darkness came, and another night.

They felt abandoned as if shipwrecked in the middle of the ocean. Everything they had been through was taking effect. They had experienced the violent attack of the storm, the shock of the loss of the Whale Rock Light, and then increasing oppressive hunger and thirst. During the storm they didn't have much time to think about what was happening. Now they had time on their hands, and, in the midst of their hunger, thirst, loneliness and desolation, their emotions of worry, bitterness, and anger grew.

Babbie, who had always loved working at the lighthouse, wanted to get out of there and never return.

About nine o'clock that night Babbie looked out toward shore and saw in the dark water, still driven by a northeast wind, a light which showed and then disappeared, then showed and disappeared again. After watching for a while, he noticed the light was moving very slowly in the direction of the lighthouse. Babbie headed for the basement.

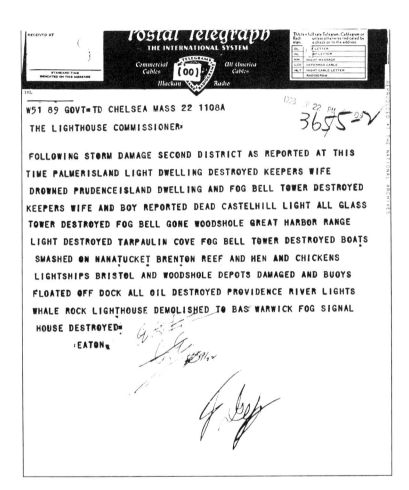

Telegram from District Superintendent George Eaton on day after the hurricane.

From the National Archives.

A little after seven o'clock that evening the Cook brothers, Jim, age 22, and Charlie, age 20, drove their Ford pickup truck alongside the pumps at Babbie's store to fill up. When they went inside they found Mrs. Babcock and Helen looking uncharacteristically glum. The two women didn't say much at first, but after the Cooks paid for the gas and some candy, the story about the lighthouse came out. By this time both mother and daughter were seriously worried that one or both of the two Plum Beach keepers might have died. They were very worked up over this point and had been trying for a good part of the day to find someone with a boat who could go out for Babbie and John.

Jim and Charlie said they could help. They had a 14 foot skiff they kept for crabbing in Pettaquamscutt River. That river, in a valley separated from the bay by the long ridge of Boston Neck, was better protected from the storm than Plum Beach had been and their boat was in fine shape.

The Cook brothers got back into their truck and rushed westward down the winding Snuff Mill Road to the shore of the upper lake where their boat was moored. When they returned to the store with the boat in the back of the pickup, Mrs. Babcock had some batteries for Charlie to put in his five-cell flashlight, and Helen gave them water to take to the two keepers.

By the time they had driven down Plum Beach Road, and down the rough right-of-way curving from the parking lot down to the beach, it was 8:30, the moon was starting to rise, and the northeast wind was still coming on strong. Quickly they pushed the boat a little ways into the breaking waves. Jim got in and grabbed the single set of oars, while Charlie pushed off and sat in the bow. Jim turned it about, and Charlie leaned forward shining the light on the three- to four-foot waves coming at them from dead ahead. Charlie and Jim Cook had taken on a real challenge.

(It is important to add, in ascribing heroism to the Cook brothers, that Charlie Cook, while describing the incident in 1984, did not view their action as heroic. He saw his brother and himself as people who discovered neighbors in need of help. "We just wanted to make them feel good," he said. Cook added "I was game, and I looked at Jim; he was game; so we did it."

As the brothers drew near the Plum Beach Light, about an hour after leaving shore, they saw two lights, a kerosene lantern burning inside, and a flashlight that Babbie was now shining down on an area of riprap on the west side where it would be safer to pull in. The light in the tower was not burning that night.

Babbie announced, "It's my turn to come in!" Actually there had been no argument. John had encouraged Babbie to go, believing he could handle things himself until further help arrived. But Babbie was most insistent that he was getting off of that light now! While Babbie made his final preparations to go home, Jim and Charie held the skiff about twenty feet off the rocks.

When Babbie joined his two rescuers in the boat, he made comments about the government being obliged to pay them for rowing out. "Of course," said Charlie, in 1984, "You know the government!" Babbie was concerned and curious as to whether any wreckage had bumped into their boat on the way out. He spoke of his fears about the cracks in the structure of the lighthouse; and he spoke about the loss of Whale Rock Light. He was most voluble and angry that the government had not rescued him and his colleague.

At the Plum Beach shore they jumped out of the skiff in a hurry to prevent capsizing the boat. It was after eleven by the time the three of them got back to the store.

The hurricane had done another kind of damage. It had driven a wedge into this usually close knit family. Babbie was restless and inconsolable. "Why didn't you do something to help us? Why didn't you send someone out to get us? We had nothing to eat, nothing to drink."

The damage to family unity was only temporary especially because Helen Babcock was as strong-minded and vocal as her father. She explained, in no uncertain terms, how bad the storm had been on land. But since he had come home at night, and since their yard had no large trees, he hadn't seen any real damage. He went to bed that night exhausted and unconvinced of their efforts at rescue.

When he got up the next morning, Babbie, mad at his family and the government, announced his intention to drive to Wickford. Helen shouted out emphatically, "You can't go to Wickford." "I'd like to know why," Babbie answered. Helen told him there was no way he could get there.

Babbie responded with indignation, "I'd like to know why I can't go to Wickford. I've been driving there all my life!" Helen tried again to explain, but Babbie took the car and headed north on Boston Neck Road.

People believe that the great volume of rain that had fallen during the four days prior to September 21 had so loosened the soil that the violent winds easily uprooted great numbers of large and venerable trees. It would be days before enough crews had come

Charles Cook, in Army uniform in early 1940's, with brother, Jim, rescued Babbie from the lighthouse following the 1938 hurricane.

Courtesy of Mr. & Mrs. Charles Cook

Assistant keeper Johnny Ganze in mid-1939 on footplates and main gallery at edge of 12-foot drop to riprap rocks. Beginnings of the original Jamestown Bridge in background.

Photo courtesy of Ganze family.

from states out of the storm's path to clear all of the state's roads and to extricate trees that had been blown into people's houses. The cleanup would take months.

Babbie was not gone long. Helen stood in the middle of the store, waiting for him as he walked in from the car. She looked right at him. "I guess," he said, breathing hard, "You folks got it as bad as we did."

Finally John Ganze was rescued. He came ashore, and got some much needed food and clothing. As he rowed back to the lighthouse that afternoon he saw the lighthouse tender anchored near the damaged lighthouse dock. When Ganze climbed up the dock, he met Superintendent George Eaton who reprimanded him for leaving the lighthouse deserted while he was ashore.

Ganze later said that right then and there he had felt like telling Eaton "You can take the lighthouse and shove it!" What he actually said was "Why weren't you here when we needed you? I was starving and couldn't drink the water." And there was no more arguing. They had to assess the damages and get the lantern working again.

A few days later Keeper Reuben Phillips appeared on the shore fresh from his vacation in Vermont where the storm had been mild. He waved, but had to wait a while for Ganze to start rowing in to shore to meet him. Phillips complained to Ganze about the delay. John replied, "Wait 'til you get out there. You'll see!" Upon reaching the lighthouse, Phillips just stood and stared.

Among the personal items Phillips reported lost or destroyed during the storm were his seven year old barometer and his radio.

Both Babbie and John Ganze continued to feel bitterness toward the government for the way they were treated during the storm. Ganze had appreciated the improvements in the supplies and administrative support for keepers which had begun with the coming of the Roosevelt administration earlier in the decade. But, in the instance of the hurricane they felt they were treated shabbily.

Over a year later they and other keepers still had not been reimbursed for food and personal property lost during the storm. Compensation would require an act of Congress! On Keeper Phillips' October 8, 1938 report listing the loss or damage of three Plum Beach keepers' personal items, the District Superintendent, Eaton, had recommended a reduction of $4.40 from the already bare-bones total request of $22.90.

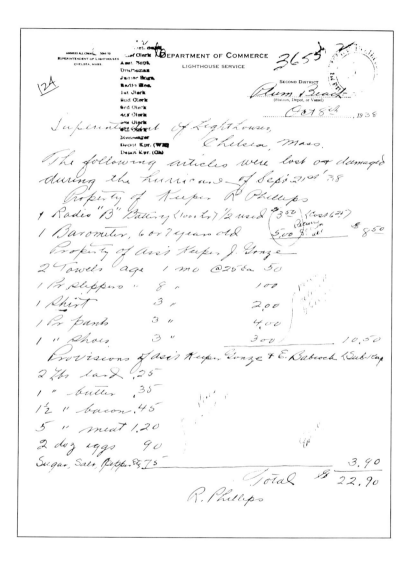

Keeper's report of personal loss and damage during hurricane shows the District Superintendent's first reduction from $22.90 to $18.50. Later he reduced it to $8.00.

From the National Archives.

When Superintendent Eaton submitted to the Commissioner in Washington his list of keepers' losses from his Second District on April 14, 1939, he had one column for "Keepers Estimate" and another one for "Superintendent's Estimate." The Plum Beach request of $22.90 had been reduced, in the "Superintendent's Estimate," to $8.00. Of twenty stations listed the Superintendent had intended giving only six the amounts they asked for. The total "Keepers Estimate" for the district was $11,342.15, and the Superintendent's was $7,148.70.

A June 16, 1939, letter from Commissioner H. D. King, responding to Congressman Charles F. Risk's request for information about keepers losses in the Second Congressional District of Rhode Island, states the policy in langauge rivaling that of Light-House Board bureaucrats of the 1880's and 90's.

> With reference to the amounts of claims which may have been received from the employees, it is proper to state that they may be subject to review so far as administrative approval may be sought, in line with the consideration usually given to claims of this character, as where the property is not such as would justify the Lighthouse Service to recommend reimbursement or the value claimed by the employee may be greater than what is thought to be the legitimate value of the articles.

That is to say "our employees are interested only in money and how they can cheat the government out of more money,"—a common rationale for the negative policies of some administrators and public boards.

Providence *Evening Bulletin* story of December 8, 1939, indicates that at least by that time keepers and survivors were still waiting for Congress to act on reimbursement for their lost and damaged property–over fourteen months after the catastrophic day.

While the failure of the Coast Guard cutter to stop for the two stranded Plum Beach Light keepers on September 22, 1938, was unacceptable to many people who knew the two keepers, it is not surprising when considering the widespread death and devastation throughout the state and the confusion and fractured communication systems in the aftermath of the storm. However, a calculated policy of disdain toward the keepers of the northeast was not so easy to excuse; it was outrageous. The *Lighthouse Service Bulletin* during the months following the storm had, in low-key fashion, honored the keepers of the northeast for their courage during the storm. But actions speak louder than words.

It seems fair to say that during the almost 90 years in which the Light-House Board, and later the Lighthouse Service, ran the nation's lighthouses and other aids to navigation, it was far more energetic and successful in addressing the issues of technological advances than in dealing with the needs and conditions of lighthouse personnel. In 1938 jobs were hard to find; many felt they needed to hold on to anything they could get. In the years since the beginning of the Light-House Board in 1852, and even in the years since 1938, significant changes have taken place in the history of labor relations. But the problem still remains: how do employees, who risk their lives for the public benefit, find justice without being piously accused of breaking a public trust in "deserting their posts," when they are faced with an intransigent bureaucracy and shortsighted public policy?

While it is not my view, it is possible to argue with some cogency that the air traffic controller, the postal worker and, in the old days, the lighthouse keeper ought to be supported entirely by financing from the commercial interests benefitting from these services, or that they should be privatized. Whether or not that should be done is not the point here. Since these services do function as a part of government, the people of the United States have an obligation to treat its employees in a just fashion. With the lack of administrative philosophy of this kind, it appears that Congressman Risk was taking some initiative in this direction.

However, in 1938, at the Whale Rock Light, it was not a case of a government employee deserting his post. The post deserted him! And the Plum Beach Light came close to doing the same thing but had held fast.

With the Whale Rock Light gone, the Plum Beach Light briefly assumed a significance which the Light-House Board of the 1880's and 1890's, and the campaigners who instigated the building of the lighthouse, never would have anticipated. Until an automated beacon was later installed on top of the ruins of the Whale Rock Light, the Plum Beach Light was, for a space of well over ten miles, the only light available to define the western edges of the channel of the West Passage.

However, the days of the Light at Plum Beach were numbered.

VI RETIREMENT, 1941

The End of an Era

DURING THE SAME WEEK that the winds and waves of the September 21, 1938 Hurricane were crashing into the Plum Beach Light, paralyzing the rest of Rhode Island and nearby states, the imminent collapse of Europe, abetted by the aggressive policies and actions of Hitler and the concessions made by Chamberlain and others, became inevitable.

On the day after the Hurricane, when Assistant Keeper, John O. Ganze, and Substitute Keeper, Edwin S. Babcock were feeling abandoned by everyone, people on shore who could get a copy of the Providence *Journal*, printed that day on the equipment of the Woonsocket *Call*, read of Czechoslovakia giving up its efforts to keep Germany out of the Sudetenland because, with England and France withdrawing support, its government said, "we were alone."

During the late thirties, the United States government gradually geared itself up to deal with the military threat engulfing Europe. More than any other reason it would be the military imperative that brought about the closing of the Plum Beach Light.

Over a number of years Plum Beach summer residents had organized an influential campaign to prevent the construction of the proposed Jamestown Bridge. However, they could not argue against the military necessity for having more reliable transportation between naval bases in the southern bay area.

And in May, 1941 the U.S. Coast Guard, which had taken over the Lighthouse Service in 1939, declared the Plum Beach Light permanently closed, nine months after the opening of the Jamestown Bridge on July 27, 1940. Local people had expected what a May 3, 1941 Providence *Journal* article announced, ". . . an inspection [by the Coast Guard] found that the warning lights on the Jamestown-

Saunderstown Bridge, particularly the green light marking the passageway under the main span, were satisfactory guides to mariners." In fact, the glare from the bright yellow lights along the entire bridge — twice as many as the pale lights burning in recent decades — was such that no one would have noticed the lighthouse even if it were still lit.

In addition to the lights on the bridge, its structure, low on the west side, with narrow openings, rising to a central span, would discourage ships that would be troubled by the shoal from getting anywhere near it. The 640 ft. wide central span, 135 feet above mean high water, was designed to direct deep-draught vessels over the deepest part of the West Passage channel.

All of this was common knowledge among people who were in or near Plum Beach at the time, even those of tender age. But there is more to the story.

In the months following the Hurricane of September, 1938, correspondence passed between the District Superintendent of the Second Lighthouse District, the Commissioner in Washington, the Secretary of Commerce, under whom the Commissioner served, and the Public Works Administration about plans for repairing, with PWA funds, the Plum Beach and other lighthouses of the District.

On October 7, 1938, a breakdown of hurricane repair costs by state and by light station was sent to the Public Works Administrator, along with the recommendation of the Secretary of Commerce. For the four states most seriously affected by the storm, New York, Connecticut, Rhode Island, and Massachusetts, the total was $765,000. Of that, the largest share, $289,550 was allocated for Rhode Island: Five of the twenty one lighthouses were allocated over $18,000, with the Watch Hill Light Station receiving $37,000. For Plum Beach the proposed $10,000 was to "repair, foundation, roof, railings, heater, cistern, landings, etc."

However, on October 19, 1938, Commissioner King apparently visiting the District office in Chelsea, Massachusetts, sent a telegram to his office in Washington suggesting a request to the PWA for "further projects." This resulted in at least $41,500 more for Rhode Island, including either $5,000 or $15,000 more for Plum Beach, depending on an interpretation of the listed amounts as being entirely new grant requests, or revisions of the earlier figures. In any case, as at Plum Beach, the work proposed was exactly what was mentioned in the earlier report. The Commissioner made it clear at the end of the telegram that the additional requests were made to help with the budgetary crisis resulting from the Hurricane.

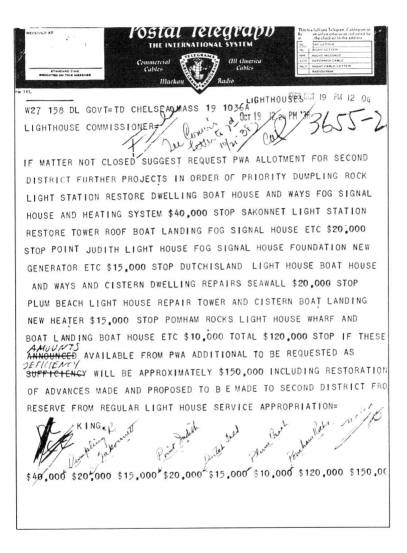

Telegram appears to up funding requests with figures padded for Plum
Beach regarding work not really intended.

From the National Archives.

What really was supposed to happen at Plum Beach came out in Superintendent Eaton's systematic report of December 30, 1938. He acknowledges that the true cost to "repair the entire structure to a quite permanent status is $13,000."

> . . .But due to the probability of the erection of a suspension type highway bridge in the near future between the mainland and Conanicut Island, it appears that the maintenance and operation of this station can be greatly modified after this bridge is completed. Therefore, it appears desirable to make only such repairs at this time as are necessary to keep the station in proper operating condition for a 5 to 10 year period. On this basis, it is recommended that only the following repairs be made at this time. . . .

The list disregards the shifting and loss of riprap stones, the reopened old cracks and the new cracks in the cast iron caisson, and the extensive cracks in the interior brick walls. The total cost of repairs under the new proposal was $4,500, instead of $15,000.

George Eaton adds, at the end of his December 30 recommendation, that he had just read in the December 29 issue of *Engineering News Record*, that the contracts had just recently been awarded for the Jamestown Bridge for an estimated $3,000,000.

The Deputy Commissioner, C.A.Park, recommended approval with the notation that Eaton's proposal was "in accord with our conference at Boston." Was that the same conference at which Commisioner King sent the October 19 telegram to his office, asking for *more* money for Plum Beach, and was he aware, then, that he wouldn't be needing the $15,000 for Plum Beach? It looked that way.

By May 2, 1939 the Deputy Commissioner had given the go ahead on a contract for the modified repair of the Plum Beach Light to William J. DuWors and Company of East Boston, Massachusetts, and during the next few months the work was almost completed.

Within a year of the awarding of the contract John Ganze would be transferred to Spectacle Island Light in Massachusetts. However, before Johnny left the Plum Beach Light, he would again be stranded at his station without a boat.

Ganze explained it this way:

> Two young guys from Boston worked [on the repairs] for about a month. When he was nearly done the man who had contracted for the job asked me if he could take the boat in and he'd come back in the morning. The job was getting pretty well completed.

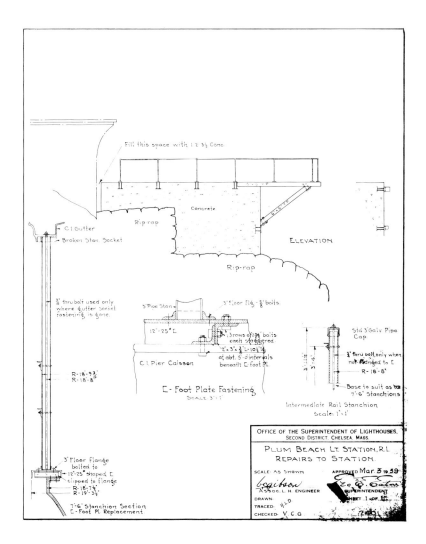

Repairs scheduled in 1939 for 130 ton concrete dock, battered and shifted in the hurricane. Some 2-4 ton riprap stones below also shifted.

From original at Governor's Island, N.Y. Courtesy of Engineering Branch, U.S.C.G. Shore Facilities Design and Construction.

He didn't come back! No boat on the beach!

Here I am out there with no boat. I bummed a ride in. I reported it at the State Police barracks. They questioned the hell out of me [as if Ganze had taken the boat]. They later found the boat in Jamestown. People came down from Boston, asked me all about the guy. They said "He's missing. So's the check. He's pulled a disappearing act."

They contacted his wife; she didn't know where he was. The man who was working for him didn't come back either.

Sometime in the first half of 1940, John Ganze was transferred to Spectacle Island Light in Massachusetts, and it was, in his words, on "very short notice." Of his leaving Plum Beach and the closing of the light, he said. "I hated like hell to go. I liked it [Plum Beach]. It was a nice place til the Hurricane came."

In June of 1941 Ganze, like other civilian lighthouse keepers, was offered the opportunity to join the Coast Guard. He accepted the offer, and received the rating of boatswain's mate second class.

While serving at Spectacle Island he became seriously ill and entered the Navy Hospital in Boston. He felt, and as his daughter later told it, it was a grave crisis, perhaps even more serious than the Hurricane. He had a growth on his head. His wife was afraid he was dying, and for a long time could not bring herself to visit. He did get a visit from the man who had replaced him at Spectacle Island who reported a rumor that Ganze had committed suicide.

After getting over the worst of his illness, and after a tense reunion with his wife, Johnny was discharged from the hospital, ending an eight month stay.

Soon after leaving the hospital Ganze took a course in welding and got a job in the Boston Navy Yard. It was there that he met the former assistant of the man who had stolen the boat from the Plum Beach Light, who told him that his former boss was now "doing time" and that he, the assistant, had never gotten paid.

Margaret Benson Ganze was, like her husband, a shy and reserved person. She was a versatile commercial artist. Margaret and Johnny shared a love of nature and rural life. Boston and the Navy Yard didn't really satisfy that kind of interest. But Johnny was a hard working, austere manager of the family budget who saved as much as he could. They looked for somewhere else to live. Babbie, with whom they had kept up a close relationship, heard that an 80 acre farm off of Snuff Mill Road was available. The farm, on the west side of the Barber's Heights hill, was owned by an alleged racketeer, and operated ostensibly as a chicken farm by a front man. On a visit to the farm they found dogs guarding the gate and a buzzer they had to push to be admitted — unlike anything else in the area.

In spite of the guarded atmosphere, the opportunity looked just right to John Ganze. His ancestors had been successful farming people in Austria and Hungary, and now he would have a try at farming himself.

In 1951 the Ganze family moved back to the area that Johnny had loved the most, back among the people who were his best friends, Babbie and his family. He worked for the Navy at Quonset Point Naval Station, but was excited about the project of making his land into a real farm. He continued to live there after his wife's death in the early 1980's, until illness sent him to a nursing home where he died in 1985.

When the Coast Guard took over the Lighthouse Service in late 1939, the timetable for closing the Plum Beach Light moved along more rapidly. George Eaton had written about the lighthouse staying open another 5 to 10 years. Forty seven years later it is impossible to say whether the Coast Guard closed it right away because of financial economy (with the imminence of war they needed all the manpower they could get) or whether it was just common sense.

However it may have been decided, the lighthouse closed with the same lack of ceremony when it opened in June of 1899. The summer people were away, and none of the long-time keepers were still involved with the light. Since the departure of Ganze, and the retirement of Reuben Phillips before, the lighthouse had been operated by two Coast Guard men. There is even some evidence that there may have been a battery operated electric lamp, during the last year, replacing the classic kerosene lamp which had burned for so many years.

The notices in the newspapers were brief and to the point. One clipping, saved by Mahlon Wright, reminds readers that the lighthouse had guided ships up the bay for 44 years (counting the years that Captain Eaton rowed out to set up the temporary light every night). The same article began, "The march of progress has spelled the doom of another lighthouse in Rhode Island," and placed the closing of Plum Beach as part of a trend. One sensed regret on the part of the author.

The coming of the bridge also doomed another institution of the West Passage, the Saunderstown-Jamestown Ferry. As in the case of the lighthouse, there simply was no practical need for it. Unlike the lighthouse, much public attention was given to that historic event. Captain Archie Arnold, who had skippered the Saunderstown Ferry for twenty three years, including the difficult September, 1938 trip we reported in Chapter V, and whose father had been quoted in the newspaper article about the *Pequot* in Chapter II, was at the wheel of the *Hammonton* for the last run on the night of Friday, July 26, 1940.

The last run was both festive and sad. At the last departure from Jamestown a huge wreath was presented to Captain Arnold, and he hung it on the front of the wheelhouse. For the last departure from Saunderstown to Jamestown a short time later, the dock at Saunderstown was loaded with well wishers waving "red fire" torches, and the *Hammonton* was loaded with her old friends, some of whom, being from the Saunderstown side, would have to wait until morning to get a ride across the bridge.

However, one old salt was absent from all this to-do about the closing of the Saunderstown Ferry. At eighty three he was considered an "old curmudgeon" by local youngsters who wanted to avoid his wrath. One old timer today remembers him as being "a hot old bird" in the 1930's and 40's. But that isn't the whole story. He was much beloved by his grandchildren and the rest of his large clan, and respected by many others for his long, strenuous service on the water.

This absentee from the excitement at the ferry dock was the first Keeper of the Plum Beach Light, Captain Joseph Lester Eaton, whom we honored for his realistic adaptation to historical shifts in Chapter I. A Providence *Journal* writer interviewed Eaton to get his perspective on the new developments for a July 25, 1940, story. He got some history from the Captain, which in the article was somewhat garbled, and then a characteristic reaction:

> But while Captain Eaton would talk of the bygone days on the ferry, he made it plain he wasn't one of the sentimentalists. Asked if he would be one of the passengers tomorrow night, he barked:
>
> "What the devil do I want to go on the boat for? I don't care anything about the last trip."

On the surface, it appears the reply was typical Eaton "barking." But he had reason to answer as he did. To begin with, this 83 year old man had seen changes which meant more to him than the closing of the Saunderstown-Jamestown Ferry.

Joseph Lester Eaton in later years.

Courtesy of Robert Eaton.

He had gained his greatest fame when, with his physical prowess and seamanship, he had single handedly operated the sailing ferry business at South Ferry. He had seen the peak of his seafaring family's fortunes back in the 1870's in South Ferry, and had watched those fortunes wane until he sold what was left and moved to Saunderstown. From a personal standpoint, if there ever was something to get emotional about, leaving South Ferry for Saunderstown in 1895 would have been it.

By 1940 Eaton had retired from most of his active involvement with the Saunderstown Ferry, and, many years earlier as a bay pilot. However, one of Eaton's activities, begun in 1897, the same year he became Keeper of the temporary light on the unfinished caisson of the Plum Beach Light, was still very much a part of his, and his family's life. The U.S. Weather Signal Station he operated had become a veritable Saunderstown institution, and a family tradition which persisted under the care of his children until 1965, eighteen years after his death at age 90 in 1947. So the termination of the Saunderstown Ferry had neither the singular significance to him that it had to others, nor did it take everything away from him.

Of course the *Journal* reporter was just doing his job in asking Captain Eaton questions about the ferries at the time of the opening of the new bridge; the issue at hand was essentially one of cross-bay transportation. However, it might have been much more interesting to get views about the changes in traffic up and down the bay during the lifetime of this man who had five decades' experience as a bay pilot.

Eaton had seen the demise of the shallow-bottomed sailing freighters, such as his family operated, and the rise of four, five, and even six masted schooners which carried several thousand tons of coal. He had seen bay traffic increase during the last two decades of the nineteenth century and peak during the early years of the twentieth.

It would appear that, in the short run at least, those who had called for improved channels and improved aids to navigation in the 1880's and 90's to benefit Providence commerce were justified. And more directly related to the Plum Beach Light story, Eaton had seen the increasing draught depth in schooners and coastal steamers make more precise marking of the channel in the West Passage a necessity, and make the Plum Beach Light a reality.

One of the ironies of the story is, however, that the very trend which brought this lighthouse in the West Passage into existence eventually made the West Passage channels obsolete. By 1903, a few years after the establishment of the Plum Beach Light, the Providence Board of Trade *Journal* was calling for dredged channels that could handle not the 25 feet called for in 1896, but ships that would draw 35 feet. For ships of that depth the East Passage was more promising. Since World War II very little has been done to maintain the West Passage as a viable channel. Given the small volume of shipping into the bay, keeping two channels open since World War II has not been realistic. And in the 1980's, a 40 foot draught is common. A channel has been kept open for originally air craft carriers and now commercial ships travelling the East Passage, around the north end of Conanicut, to Quonset Point.

The nightly New York boats down the West Passage had ceased in the early thirties, and the last of the passenger lines going to New York, the Colonial Line, used the East Passage. However, World War II brought that line and the elegant travel of an earlier era to an end. For a number of years in the forties and fifties, the *Naugatuck* offered a daily summertime schedule from Providence to Block Island — probably the last regularly scheduled passenger route in the West Passage.

Captain Joseph L. Eaton could have written a book on all he had seen and known when he disdained to participate in the ceremonious last run of the Saunderstown-Jamestown Ferry. But because of his direct involvement in the history we have just surveyed, we might say he was the book.

———————————

While many were sad about the closing of the ferry and the lighthouse, not everyone opposed the building of the new bridge. For year-round residents of Jamestown the new bridge meant more opportunities for employment, business ventures, shopping, and an easier means of dealing with medical emergencies. For people on both sides of the bridge the likelihood of winter weather curtailing travel to and from Jamestown was lessened.

But there was a group, summer people at Plum Beach and others, who not only didn't like the new bridge, but had actively worked to prevent such a thing happening.

The worst that can be said about this opposition was that there was occasionally a moderate degree of tension between neighbors, and within families, on the question of the bridge, and one individual who continued to have strong feelings about the opposition to his own involvement in the bridge project.

When Irving Hazard, heir to the farm established by Jeremiah Hazard in 1767, decided to lease his dock and buildings at the South end of Plum Beach to the Merrit-Chapman & Scott Corporation, major contractors for the new bridge, he found himself the target of a storm of complaint from some Plum Beach residents and their lawyers. They didn't like having bridge workers quartered at the Quarry, and using the dock as a staging area for sending supplies to the bridge on lighters and barges. Actually, his father, Wilbur, had provided services to Toomey, the contractor finishing the lighthouse in 1898-99.

Irving Hazard told this to me in an interview for this book approximately a year before his death in 1986. He never revealed which Plum Beach residents were trying to prevent his project. It is conceivable that some who were disappointed in their failure to prevent the bridge from happening, made Hazard the target for their wrath.

The best that can be said about the movement to oppose the bridge is that it very likely caused significant modifications in the bridge plans which lessened the impact the bridge had on the ecology of the Plum Beach community, the shore, and the bay.

The identity of the leaders of this opposition to the Jamestown bridge was well known by Plum Beachers. Two leaders, Nathan M. Wright, Jr. and Abel Reynolds, because of their actions and ideas, fit into the story of the Plum Beach Light. They had been long time friends and neighbors on Dewey Street in Providence, as well as summer neighbors at Plum Beach.

A meeting to discuss opposition to the bridge was held in Nathan Wright's office at 85 Westminster Street in Providence. As Wright described it to the author, over thirty years later, representatives of the federal government had come from Washington to listen to objections to the bridge.

Some of the issues discussed were the rumored intentions of the bridge planners to make North Road, which runs parallel to Plum Beach Road, the main approach to the bridge, and the intentions of the planners to have a solid causeway partway across the bay where the level portion of the bridge is now. Abel Reynolds was short, and in his old age, stout. He was known for speaking animatedly. One of the men from Washington was tall. As Nathan Wright recalled it,

Nathan M. Wright, Jr. crossing Dorrance Street in Providence.

Courtesy of the Wright Family.

Reynolds stood up in a chair and shook his finger near the Washington man's face to emphasize his argument.

Several of Reynolds' grandchildren have since refuted the story, saying that their grandfather actually pulled that stunt at a party in Wright's house. However, the story illustrates how strongly Reynolds, a spirited man, was involved in the campaign. In any case the battle over the issues of the causeway and the bridge road was won, although they ultimately lost the war against the bridge.

One of the arguments against the bridge remembered by Nathan's son, Mahlon, was if the bridge were to be bombed in wartime, the wreckage would block the channel on the West Passage. Eventually, however, the need for dependable transportation between the island bases and the mainland proved to be the stronger argument.

One of the more interesting arguments came from Abel Reynolds, who did a lot more than just shake his finger at his opponents. John Bradner, in his unpublished *Some Memories and Some History of Plum Beach*, cited in Chapter IV, refers to "an old survey that showed quicksand in the Bay," and explained that Abe Reynolds argued that it would be unsafe to build across the Plum Beach Shoal.

In the 1930's someone remembered Col. Ludlow's borings of 1896! Abe Reynolds would have been old enough to have read the February 8, 1897 *Journal* article quoted in Chapter III. He was also a shrewd politician and businessman, at that time serving as Vice President and General Manager of New England Waterworks. Family members see him as a person with a sharp memory who, even if he had not remembered the story of Ludlow's borings, would have followed every possible angle to win his cause and would have initiated research to see if the documentation about establishing the foundation in the shoal could be of any help to their cause. In any case John Bradner tells us Reynolds sent to Washington for the data.

Had Reynolds succeeded, with his argument, in preventing the building of the Jamestown bridge, this book would have turned out differently, and we could say that the Plum Beach Light had "saved" itself. However, there is the possibility that the data from the old borings might have made the designers of the bridge more sensitive to the challenges that lay within the layers of the Plum Beach Shoal.

For the section of the 1940 bridge built over the Plum Beach Shoal on the west side of the central span, the method of construction was similar to the original design for the construction of the 1992 bridge, in that the foundations of the piers on the west side of the main channel were not designed to go down to bed rock but to be supported deep in the layers of sand. It involved the use of coffer dams and the driving of piles of timber and of concrete and steel deep into the shoal. A contemporary news article by Leonard O. Warner explains the construction:

> . . .On the west end, near the mainland, the ledge drops too far down to pour concrete directly on it. There the procedure for building the coffer dams is the same [as on the east side], but the method of constructing piers much more difficult.
>
> For 20 piers on the west end, hundreds of long timbers ranging from 60 to 90 feet long are brought along side a lighter-derrick in a scow. The timbers, as many as 240 in one coffer dam, are driven into the mud side-by-side and one-by-one beneath the water until the tops are at least 42 feet below the surface.
>
> ### Piles Driven Down
>
> The mass timber piles are not driven to the ledge, but only as far as the engineer thinks is deep enough to withstand the load of the bridge and its traffic. In one coffer dam, and only one, steel piles were driven one-by-one until they struck the ledge.
>
> Once the piles are driven, the diver goes down under to cut off the ends of those that stick out. Some, of course, stick up higher than others, depending on how deep each goes before striking ledge or a boulder. . .

The extensive article goes on to explain the pouring of concrete under water right on top of the piles, followed by sealing and pumping dry the inside of the coffer dam, in which a large concrete pier is then built up on top of the base of piles. While the article begs the question of inconsistencies about the boulders and ledges, it deals with a highly technical subject which has baffled people with a greater technical background than the author of this book.

What stands out most strongly is the engineer's responsibility: "only as far as the engineer thinks is deep enough to withstand the load. . . ." This explanation tacitly acknowledges the uncertainties of building on the Plum Beach Shoal, and the issue of professional authority .pressed by Ludlow in 1896. With the more complex process of construction in the 1980's in mind, the reference to the engineer's responsibility, in 1939, anticipates the issue of proper analysis of material from borings in the Plum Beach Shoal in preparation for the successor to the 1940 bridge.

Apparently E. L. MacDonald, the Chief Engineer, and William H. Bruce, the Resident Engineer, did their job well in establishing the bridge foundation in the shoal. With all the complaints about the condition of the old bridge in recent years, no one has raised the issue of the stability of the bridge's footing in the ground under the bay.

Beyond all the arguments of the bridge opponents, and they were many, what did they really want? While it is somewhat presumptuous to assess the motives of people whose campaign fifty years ago largely failed, several points stand out:

Some opponents of the bridge suspected that it would fail financially. Not enough people would want to use it, and the income from tolls wouldn't be enough to pay the remaining debt. Not anticipating the wartime use that would begin in a few years, and the advantage motorists would find in cutting off the route through Providence to go from New York to Cape Cod, they called it "The Bridge to Nowhere." They feared, as reported in a New York *Times* article of July 7, 1940, that the burden of the debt would fall on the State of Rhode Island. Perhaps some of the opponents, politically conservative, saw the bridge as another mistake of Roosevelt's New Deal. And the value of property may have been another concern.

The Plum Beach summer people who opposed the bridge had other reasons even stronger than their financial and political ones. They came to Plum Beach every year because they loved the bay, the hillside, and the islands across the bay. They feared that the bridge would alter their treasured vacation spot. Even if a bridge had to be built, they thought the design of this one was ugly. Abel Reynolds' daughter, Louise Reynolds Bradner, three decades after the bridge opened, continued to call it "That obscene bridge."

Those opposed felt that the bridge traffic would have a bad effect on the community. And they worried that the bridge, going across Plum Beach Point, would devastate the beauty of the pond and tidal marshes on the point, and on the Beach Club land just south of the point.

Most of these worries turned out to be partly justified, and in some respects entirely justified. Whatever one may think about the Bridge, it did alter the ecology of the point and the landscape for miles around. One unexpected surprise was, as people drove around the Boston Neck area and Conanicut, the bridge kept appearing on the horizon in unexpected places; its appearance looked refreshingly different from each vantage point.

But something else was lost with the coming of the bridge, something more elusive than the view of the bay, or the impact of traffic. What was lost was a way of life, the world of the lower West Passage in the first few decades of the century. And very likely the Hurricane and World War II, both having a strong impact on the area, had as much to do with this sense of loss as the coming of the bridge.

Some of the bridge opponents sensed early on an impending loss. And, even though the battle seemed hopeless, what they treasured was worth fighting for.

What was to be lost was a relaxed, peaceful intimacy with the larger environment of the bay, an involvement with it, and thus a measure of control and order to their lives.

And the two symbols which brought this view of life into the strongest focus, the Plum Beach Light and the Saunderstown-Jamestown Ferry, would be eliminated by the bridge.

Perhaps a custom treasured in memory by Nathan Wright's family illustrates the way people lived before the coming of the bridge. Mahlon Wright explained that his father, Nathan, and his grandfather, Mahlon Gowdy, often went for a game of golf at the Beavertail Golf Club on a Saturday or Sunday morning in the summer. Around noon his mother would be standing on the porch looking out onto the bay.

> . . .Before all these trees grew up, Mother would plan to put the corn on when she saw a hand-mirror signal from the ferry which meant that Grampa and Dad were aboard, they're on their way back, and she knew it would take them from the time they flashed the mirror. . .she could go to work and put whatever had ten or fifteen minutes to go to have lunch. . .and you know how methodical she was. . .string beans or corn or whatever had to be cooked. . .

Imagine the scene on the ferry! The two men might emerge from their car by the time the ferry had pulled out of the West Ferry slip of Jamestown village. As the ferry headed northwest around the north side of Dutch Island, they would stand by the rail on the north side of the ferry and look at the hill at Plum Beach over a mile away.

People on the ferry deck would look in wonder at Nate Wright as he flashed the hand mirror. After putting it back into his pocket he would pull a fine cigar out of another pocket, clip off a piece from one end, and light it. He probably enjoyed this part of the morning as much as the golf game. He would look up and down the bay, savoring, almost simultaneously, the odor of the cigar and the ocean air. Leaning one arm on the high rail of the ferry and occasionally hooking a thumb behind his suspenders, he would take satisfaction at their cleverness in thinking up the mirror communication scheme. Calling his father-in-law by his first name, he would comment on the way other players on the golf course had behaved. While talking, he would pull out the mirror one more time just to make sure.

A woman standing nearby might approach and ask him about the mirror. Nathan Wright would raise slightly the brim of his straw hat, and smile broadly. In rare form now, regardless of what may have happened on the golf course, he would tell about the scheme with pleasure, and with style.

That was the life!

With today's fast pace and the domination of the automobile, we have a much different view of the bay, and our relation to it.

Then there was an intimate connection with the environment. The ferry captains, before radar, would guide their ships safely through thick fog by listening to the echoes of their tooted whistle. The sound, and timing of the reverberation would tell them where they were. When you looked out and saw the lighthouse turn on, you knew that the keeper was a master of the challenging currents of the bay, and they were known for personally assisting boaters in trouble.

———————————————

The newspaper accounts of the August 27, 1940 lineup of cars at the toll house at the Plum Beach end of the Jamestown bridge are confusing, because what happened was confusing. There was a bit of a scramble among drivers wanting to be the first to cross the new bridge and Nathan Wright's wife and two sons were part of it. Waldo Wright believes the articles had many details wrong, especially the parts alleging his father was there. But the newspapers didn't miss the irony that Waldo's father who had been "a bitter opponent of the bridge from the outset. . .and sought to oppose it in Washington," would be involved in the opening day of the bridge. .

Nathan Wright had been accustomed to the idea that a person could make his influence felt. His father had, for years, been one of the most prominent leaders of the state Republican party. Nathan, Jr., was president of his own firm, Mortgage Guarantee & Title Company, and was also a lawyer. He had a gift for verbal expression that was honed by his years at Classical High School in Providence, Brown University, and Boston University Law School. He was known for always pulling the precise word out of his extensive vocabulary, and for spontaneously fashioning a resonant, incisive, sentence. He was usually very formal, but he had the ability to use language to express an almost unctuous graciousness, gruff bluntness, raucous humor, tumultuous anger, and tenderness.

If anyone could have stopped the building of the Jamestown Bridge, Nate Wright, Abe Reynolds and their associates would have been the ones to do it. But in the face of the federal administration's plans for a network of highways in southern New England the campaign to stop the bridge was as hopeless as Canute's legendary efforts to hold back the oncoming tide!

The Bridge was now open and operating, but Nathan M. Wright, Jr., had not finished his war with the bridge.

We have already discussed how the bridge took over the mission of the lighthouse as a <u>visual</u> aid to navigation; we have not mentioned the fog signal. The fog bell in the Plum Beach Light was replaced by a siren placed in the superstructure over the main span of the bridge. It was controlled by the staff in the tollbooth at Plum Beach Point. The signal sounded like the siren on a fire truck or a World War II air raid signal. The loud signal was of long duration and repeated at frequent intervals. Sometimes fog has been known to settle in for several days and nights at a time. And since the tollbooth keepers were almost a mile away from the main channel they were not always sure how thick the fog was, and tended to turn it on at the slightest sign of fog.

Nate Wright was a light sleeper, at best; when the siren was going at night, he claimed that he couldn't sleep at all, especially if the siren got neighborhood dogs barking. We won't quote the epithets and expletives he used in describing and defining the source of his suffering, nor mention the kinds of sick animals he compared it to, but his complaints succeeded in getting the volume and style of the siren altered.

———————————————

For Edwin S. Babcock, the lighthouse, as he knew and loved it, was lost on the afternoon of September 21, 1938, when the Hurricane struck. We have no indication that he regretted the official closing of the light in 1941. His former associates had already gone. Keeper Reuben Phillips had retired to his farm in Lafayette and worked as a janitor for the Lafayette School. (The late Avis Phillips (no relation), who taught at that school, knew him to be a kindly person much loved by students.) And Babbie's good friend, Assistant Keeper Johnny Ganze, had already been transferred to Spectacle Island, Massachusetts.

Aside from the devastating experience at the lighthouse during the Hurricane, the changes occuring between 1938-1941 were favorable to Babbie and his family. The wartime buildup of navy bases in Rhode Island brought them significant new business opportunities, and the necessity of working harder than ever.

Even the Hurricane proved to be beneficial for the family. A few days after the storm, a crew of men from New York State, answering ads offering fifty cents an hour for able bodied men who could swing an axe arrived to clean up south county properties covered with trees felled during the Hurricane. Enoch L. Dwelly, well known since as Bill Dwelly, was one of them. His brother was another. They and others stayed in the cabins at Babbie's. Not only did they eat meals at Babbie's, they also had lunches brought by Helen to the work site.

Bill and Helen Babcock fell in love, and subsequently married. During the next twenty years they made a major contribution to the success of the family business. Bill Dwelly was mellower than his sometimes blunt father-in-law, but respected Babbie's instincts, good business sense, and sense of community service. He was a dedicated Saunderstown volunteer fireman, and Helen was active in that Association, too. Like Helen's parents Bill and Helen were active in Odd Fellows and Rebekahs and rose to the highest statewide leadership. In 1960 they bought out the business from Helen's parents, and following Babbie's death in 1969 took on a major expansion.

Before leaving Babbie and his tradition, two brief scenes which convey the lasting impact of the hurricane adventure in the Plum Beach Light:

In 1951 I had a friend from Providence visiting. In the course of the visit we took an evening walk to Babbie's for soda. Babbie was usually around the store in the evenings, and wanting to impress my guest, I pointed to Babbie and said "this man was in the lighthouse during the Hurricane." Babbie was obviously pleased to have that event remembered, and, with a little encouragement, launched into extensive narrative while the three of us sat at the family table by the door.

Babbie (Edwin S. Babcock) in later years still spoke with vigor and feeling about his adventure at the lighthouse in the 1938 hurricane.

Courtesy of Bill and Helen Dwelly.

What stands out from that encounter 13 years after the Hurricane, are the fear and horror Babbie rekindled from the past, and his sense of pride about having survived, and having been a part of such an exciting and notable event.

In 1984, 45 years after the Hurricane, I attended a lecture by G. Edward Prentice on the Old Sea View Railroad (for which Babbie had worked). I introduced myself to Bill Arnold, one of the few surviving Sea View employees. All I said was that I had grown up at Plum Beach and had known Babbie.

His immediate response was, "Yes! He was in the lighthouse during the Hurricane."

————————————

And now we come to the most unpleasant part of the story at the Plum Beach Light. What happened to the structure?

The Hurricane, the Bridge and the War had brought changes that were irreversible. The lighthouse, which represented a way of life on the bay, would never reopen.

But the structure itself, sunken cast iron, concrete-filled caisson, riprap, conical shaped tower, galleries, and lantern deck, remains standing to this day.

Something must be said about jurisdiction of the lighthouse. Both in 1895 and 1933 Lighthouse Distict officials questioned the national lighthouse headquarters about whether the State of Rhode Island had officially made "cession of jurisdiction and ownership of the site of the lighthouse" to the federal government. But from archival evidence and Coast Guard legal experts we learn that cession of jurisdiction was never requested because of the paramount right of the government to regulate commerce and safeguard navigation in navigable waters even while the state retains ownership of the territory.

Whatever the legal ramifications, the functional jurisdiction has shifted back and forth. In 1957, the Coast Guard formally abandoned the property, according to a letter to Senator William Proxmire from Captain F. M. Fisher, Jr., the Coast Guard's Congressional Liaison Officer, and informed the General Services Administration of its action. By September 23, 1970 the State Department of Natural Resources was in control, and advertised it for leasing for the first time. William F. A. Bryant, writing for the Newport *Daily News* on that date, quotes D.N.R.'s Chief of Harbors and Rivers, Henry Ise, as saying that the state had received the lighthouse about 15 years prior, and, contrary to local stories, had never been up for rent or sale before.

Before, during, and after the 1970 bidding, offers regarding its use have been made by a fishing club, by Radio Station WKFD for promotional purposes, by many individuals for private purposes, and by Raytheon Corporation, which offered $1,000 a year and $20,000 worth of renovation and repair so that they could use it for research.

By 1983 D.N.R. had become the Department of Environmental Management; and the Department was preparing to sell the lighthouse. (The newspaper article at that time misnamed the structure which prompted me to write this history.) Sometime between 1983 and 1987 the Coast Guard resumed functional control of the structure.

The 1970 efforts of the Department of Natural Resources to lease the building were forestalled by the discovery that a U. R. I. Zoology graduate student had been using, and would continue to use, the lighthouse for research on the nesting habits of pigeons. Aside from the fact that people have fished near there for years (apparently the riprap attracts the fish), the pigeon study is the only practical use of the lighthouse since 1941.

U.R.I. Zoology Professor Frank Heppner, who supervised the 1970 research project, heard about D.N.R.'s plans to paint the lighthouse, we are told in a December 15, 1983 *Standard-Times* article. He warned the Department of the danger of contracting the serious disease histoplasmosis from contact with the dust of bird feces. Apparently not enough caution was taken. As chronicled in a March, 1984 Providence *Journal* artricle, James Osborn filed suit against the State when he allegedly contracted the pulmonary and ocular types of the fungal disease while painting the lighthouse for the state. He stated that he was blind in one eye, and was advised he would go blind in the other. Final resolution of this suit is still pending.

Because cleaning up hardened layers of bird feces several feet thick throughout the inside of the lighthouse presented an overwhelming challenge, causing one contractor to withdraw from the job, the Coast Guard discontinued recent cleanup efforts. Captain F. M Hamilton, Group Commander at Woods Hole, told me in early 1988, when I made a request to visit the lighthouse, that the risk of illness was too great, and intended to seal all of the openings against birds or people getting in.

In May of 1988 the Coast Guard reconsidered its legal relationship to the old structure and concluded "that the Plum Beach lighthouse is unquestionably the property of the State of Rhode Island" with the explanation that the land under the bay had always belonged to the state and that the structure became the property of the state when it was abandoned in 1958.

In 1984 The University of Rhode Island made a comprehensive study of the Plum Beach Light, with an interest in moving it to the Bay Campus at South Ferry. Kenneth Morse, of the U.R.I. Library Reference faculty, well versed in lighthouse history, visited the Plum Beach structure, and was impressed with the brickwork arcade in the basement. More recently, consideration was given to the idea of moving the structure and including it in the plans for India Point Park in Providence. However, the cast iron concrete-filled caisson foundation presents a serious problem for anyone planning to move it.

But I did get in once, many years ago. My neighbor and friend, Bob, said one fall day when few people were around, "Let's go out to the lighthouse!" He suggested taking the Club's skiff, which had not been put away for the winter. With a mixture of fear and eagerness, I agreed. There was no question about who would row, he being a far better rower than I.

We soon pulled the boat onto one of the pieces of riprap at water level, and proceeded to look around. How could we get in? The gallery deck was about 10-12 feet above the riprap. Then we saw the south basement porthole about 6 feet above us. I was still scared, but not Bob. "Give me a boost," he said, " and then I'll pull you up." I can still feel the scraping on my ribs and visualize the brown marks on my skin where I was pulled through the tight, slightly rusty opening.

We were in the basement. It seemed larger than I had expected, and mostly empty, with a few small pools of water here and there on the concrete floor. We quickly looked into a few of the smaller chambers in the basement, then climbed the spiral staircase to the kitchen level. This was not the impressive immaculate building that my forebears had visited in 1915. The kitchen was dirty too. And I was still afraid. I was afraid that the boat might float away, and the claustrophobia induced by this strange place was ironic, considering how much I had always enjoyed looking at the lighthouse.

Charcoal sketch of Plum Beach Light by Margaret Benson Ganze, wife of the Assistant Keeper. Shows winch apparatus on dock and basement porthole through which author climbed in 1948.

Courtesy of Alda Kaye.

However, I saw one thing in the old lighthouse that was still beautiful, and I doubt if my readers would guess what it was. On the east side of the basement deck a small door leads to the washroom. And there, still there, in this structure from which all other meaningful equipment had been removed, on in its proper place on top of the toilet bowl, was an unpainted wooden toilet seat covered with shiny clear varnish that revealed the beautiful grain of the wood. I had never seen a wooden toilet seat that was <u>not painted</u>, and I haven't seen many since. I was impressed. There in the most humble, but very important, part of the lighthouse its former glory remained.

Now the glory of the Plum Beach Light is hard to see. Through the years the exterior has become more and more delapidated. The roof of the main gallery has just about all fallen in. It needs paint badly. Perhaps only those of us who can still visualize its former beauty can see anything good about it at all.

The lighthouse is like the seriously ill patient who just won't die, and people say "has a good heart"; it has a structural strength worth noting. Terry Cramer, a staff member at the Coast Guard Aids to Navigation office in Boston, told me in a telephone conversation several years before this book was published, that after inspecting the Plum Beach and other discontinued stations in New England, he found Plum Beach to be in better condition than many of them, including Deer Island (Boston Harbor).

When you consider that the cracks in the cast iron caisson, the cast iron superstructure, and the interior masonry were never repaired, that nothing has been repaired since 1941, but only painted a few times, that since the 1938 Hurricane there was a milder one in 1944, and then powerful Hurricane Carol in 1954, which destroyed the Club building just as the '38 had done, you have to admire the way this pneumatic caisson lighthouse, as a building, has survived. Credit must go to the engineers, the builders, the Light-House Board, and others who saw to protection during the forty four years it operated.

As this book is going to the printer, recurring questions about the ownership of the lighthouse and initiatives of a Massachusetts company to remove the structure to that state have provoked the organizing of a new group dedicated to preserving the Plum Beach Light in its present location.

I heartily support these efforts but with the attitude that a refurbished structure will be a monument to something that, essentially, is no longer to be found. The wisdom and courage of the engineers and builders cannot be *restored*. The activity, the way of life, centered on the lighthouse cannot be *restored*. The adventure, courage, and suffering of John Ganze, Babbie, and the Cook brothers cannot be *restored*. The way the community once enjoyed the lighthouse cannot be *restored*. The vital commerce up and down the West Passage in the 1890's cannot be *restored*.

But the story of the lighthouse need not be forgotten. It can be claimed as part of our heritage.

APPENDIX A

Chronology of the Construction of Rhode Island Lighthouses by Kenneth Morse

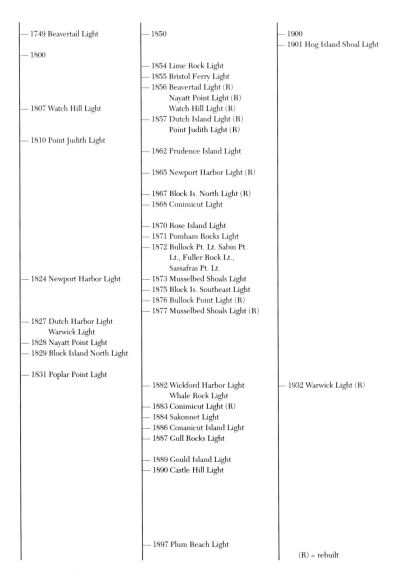

— 1749 Beavertail Light

— 1800

— 1807 Watch Hill Light

— 1810 Point Judith Light

— 1824 Newport Harbor Light

— 1827 Dutch Harbor Light
        Warwick Light
— 1828 Nayatt Point Light
— 1829 Block Island North Light

— 1831 Poplar Point Light

— 1850

— 1854 Lime Rock Light
— 1855 Bristol Ferry Light
— 1856 Beavertail Light (R)
        Nayatt Point Light (R)
        Watch Hill Light (R)
— 1857 Dutch Island Light (R)
        Point Judith Light (R)

— 1862 Prudence Island Light

— 1865 Newport Harbor Light (R)

— 1867 Block Is. North Light (R)
— 1868 Conimicut Light

— 1870 Rose Island Light
— 1871 Pomham Rocks Light
— 1872 Bullock Pt. Lt. Sabin Pt.
        Lt., Fuller Rock Lt.,
        Sassafras Pt. Lt.
— 1873 Musselbed Shoals Light
— 1875 Block Is. Southeast Light
— 1876 Bullock Point Light (R)
— 1877 Musselbed Shoals Light (R)

— 1882 Wickford Harbor Light
        Whale Rock Light
— 1883 Conimicut Light (R)
— 1884 Sakonnet Light
— 1886 Conanicut Island Light
— 1887 Gull Rocks Light

— 1889 Gould Island Light
— 1890 Castle Hill Light

— 1897 Plum Beach Light

— 1900
— 1901 Hog Island Shoal Light

— 1932 Warwick Light (R)

(R) = rebuilt

Courtesy of Kenneth Morse.

168

APPENDIX B

The Eleven U. S. Lighthouses Constructed by the Pneumatic Caisson Method
(Chapters II and III)

NAME	LOCATION	COMPLETED
Fourteen Foot Bank	Westerly side main channel, lower Delaware Bay	1886
Wolf Trap	Virginia	1894
Solomons Lump	Maryland	1895
Smith Point	Virginia	1897
Plum Beach	Narragansett Bay, Rhode Island	1899
Hooper Island	Easterly side, Chesapeake Bay, Maryland	1902
Point No Point	Maryland	1902
Sabine Bank	Louisiana	1906
Baltimore	Maryland	1908
Elbow of Cross Ledge	New Jersey	1910
Thimble Shoal	Chesapeake Bay, northerly side of channel to Hampton Roads, Virginia	1914

There are 36 others using iron caisson method <u>without</u> the pneumatic caisson technology. All of the 36 are on the east coast, from Maine to Virginia.

Information compiled from The United States Lighthouse Service-1923, compiled by John S. Conway, Deputy Commissioner of Lighthouses, Government Printing Office, 1923 and from The Annual Lists of Aids to Navigation for the applicable years.

APPENDIX C

Equipment Used in Constructing Pneumatic Caisson Foundation of Fourteen Foot Bank Light
(Chapter III)

1. A locomotive boiler, with 18 square feet of grate and 400 square feet of heating surface, and carrying 60 pounds pressure: this proved too small

2. A feed pump, connecting with the hot-well of the surface-condenser, with the fresh-water tanks and with the sea.

3. A surface-condenser, connected with all the engines and pumps.

4. A 2-cylinder hoisting-engine, with cylinders 6 1/2 inches in diameter and 9 inches stroke; the diameter of the rope-drum was 16 inches, and was geared to the engine ratio of 1 to 5.

5. A Delameter air-compressor, having 2 steam-cylinders of 8 inches diameter, and air cylinders, 10 inches diameter and 16 inches stroke. A maximum velocity of 120 revolutions per minute was required to blow the sand out of the caisson.

6. A Clayton air-compressor of the same capacity as the one above named; this was used to relieve the other while under repair. Both compressors were provided with water-jackets around their cylinders. The air was forced through water in a cylindrical cooler 2 feet 9 inches in diameter and 5 feet 4 inches high, and through a 2 1/2 inch rubber hose, to the upper end of the air shaft. Gauges on the cooler indicated the water-level in it and the air pressure. There was a check-valve also where the air entered the shaft. The air in the air-lock and in the upper part of the shaft became intensely hot, because no provision had been made for circulating water through the cooler; the workmen suffered considerably on this account.

7. A portable centrifugal pump, with 4-inch suction and discharge, and connected to the boiler and surface-condenser with hose. This pump was used as a bilge pump.

8. A duplicate of the above was used to furnish water for mixing concrete.

9. An air-lock large enough to admit 4 men at one time; it was made of boiler-iron, and had a cast iron cylinder supply-lock of one cubic yard's capacity.

From pages 148-149 of *Lighthouses Ancient and Modern*, by Major D. P. Heap.

APPENDIX D

Providence *Journal* article, February 8, 1897
(Chapter III)

PLUM BEACH LIGHT

**Substructure Completed and Appropriation Exhausted.
Some $10,000 of $15,000 were needed for the Lighthouse**

How the Work Has Been Done and What Caused the Excess
of Cost Over the First Estimate—Speedy Action
of Congress Hoped For.

The sub-structure upon which will be erected the lighthouse off Plum Beach in the West Passage of Narragansett Bay is now finished, but when the latter portion of the structure will be completed and the light established to cheer the mariner who navigates these waters is problematical, owing to a disease that not infrequently affects the progress of construction of public work, the sudden practical exhaustion of the fund granted for the purpose by legislative bodies.

In this instance, Congress at its last session appropriated the sum of $60,000. for the carrying out of the project, under the supposition that the amount was adequate for the construction of the sub and superstructures, and had it not become obligatory to sink the foundation some feet lower than was at first intended, thereby necessitating an additional expenditure up to the practical extinction of the sum granted, this supposition appears to have been well founded, for in due time a Philadelphia firm, accustomed to work of that sort, took a contract for the entire work as laid out by the Lighthouse Board's plans and specifications.

The general direction of the affair having been placed in the hands of Lieut. Col. Ludlow's corps of engineers in command of this district, F. C. Arthur, the Philadelphia people's supervising contractor, began early last summer in Providence the building of a caisson formed of heavy timber, whose exterior was 35 feet square and heighth 10 feet 8 inches, that was to be used in connection with the submerging of the hollow iron cylinder, which would constitute the real foundation of the new lighthouse, and by September the caisson was in a condition to be floated down the bay to its destination off Plum Beach, where, after securing to it in an upright position several continuous sections of the hollow iron pillar, whose diameter was 33 feet, the combined mass was sunk to the bottom of the bay, which at that point showed a depth of 17 feet at mean low water.

The next procedure in order was the filling of the interior of the cylinder with a concrete consisting of a Portland cement and selected stones and sand, leaving only what is denominated a working chamber at the bottom of the cylinder, whose dimensions were 29 feet square, with a height of six feet eight inches, and a shaft running through the centre of the iron enclosure five feet in diameter, furnished with an iron ladder, which formed a means of communication with the working chamber and the uppermost iron pipe that held the machinery and that rose above the water several feet. The outside of this section of the huge pipe or iron cylinder had suspended from it on the outside another ladder,which served as a connecting link between those on the substructure and the outside world, who were conveyed to and from the mainland in steam or sailing craft. The erection of this portion of the structure and its sinking required a gang of over 20 men with a lighter upon which were the cement and other supplies, the lighter being moored for convenience close to the work in progress, besides the constant attendance of a small steamer like the Anawon and later tug Aquidneck and steam lighter Archer.

Everything being in readiness and United States inspector John Gartland, who looked after the Government's interests on the spot, having pronounced the material used and the execution of the undertaking satisfactory, the second and most difficult portion of the task, the penetration of the successive strata at the bay's bottom, a distance of about 23 feet, was next in order. To do this, navvies, many of whom were skilled in the work, had to descend by the air shaft in the center of the cylinder, whose outer edges rested in the black mud of the first stratum, and with shovels and other implements begin the excavation for the gradual lowering of the structure, aided by pneumatic power in the form of compressed air of an average pressure of 22 to 23 pounds to the square inch, that gave a gross pressure at the first named figure of something like 1276 tons or upward, leaving a net weight of about 1500 tons.

The loosening of the several stratas of mud, sand, and gravel went smoothly and expeditiously on, and it was removed by a pneumatic device demominated a blow pipe about four inches in diameter, that carried up the mud and other debris as fast as supplied by the workmen. The operation of the blow pipe was regulated by a valve, and its force was such that the material it conveyed upward to the topmost cylinder was discharged over the surface of the water a distance of about 200 feet from the work under construction. The rapidity of the execution of this portion of the work can be realized when it is stated that between the blasts, which were only about 20 seconds in duration, but one minute and a half usually intervened.

The caisson having finally reached to within about two feet of the depth required by the contract with the substruction, being at that time lodged on a bed of sand and gravelly formation, it was thought advisable by Lieut. Col Ludlow to bore down a few feet lower, in order to ascertain of what substance the underlying stratum consisted. This resulted in disclosing the somewhat unpleasant fact that the caisson was only some two feet above a bed of quicksand, and as a matter of course, if the sinking stopped at the contract depth, the lighthouse foundation would be of that unstable material, while subsequent borings showed that after passing the stratum, which was four feet in thickness, one foot of loose sand was reached, and beneath it a hard sand bottom of ample depth and consistency to support the foundation and the superstructure.

Under the circumstances the engineer officer at once ordered Mr. Arthur to suspend operations and Lieut. Col. Ludlow, accompanied by the contractor, paid a visit to the headquarters of the Lighthouse Board in Washington, and the state of affairs being laid before them, the members decided that the caisoon, with its cylinder, must be sunk an additional seven feet to the sand bottom. In order to accomplish this within the limits of the sum appropriated, it was further determined, with the aquiescence of the contractors, to relieve the firm of the erection of the lighthouse proper. by which action the funds required for the continued construction of the foundation were made available.

This labor has now been performed and was accepted a few days ago by the Superintendent of this lighthouse district, when Mr. Arthur had filled the top of the bell section with sand and covered it with a wooden roof. This section will eventually have to be removed by the new contractor or whoever builds the superstructure, as an extra section of straight cylinder will have to be added. The present structure will be illuminated day and night by a light suspended from an arm that is fastened to an upright spar placed in the centre of the wooden roof.

The completed substructure now stands from its cutting edge on the hard sands to the wooden roof, surmounting the bell or trumpet-shaped section 59 feet in height, its total weight being 2900 tons and as a still further protection to that portion of the iron cylinder that reaches from the beginning of the first penetration of the bottom to the water above, these exposed sections have been surrounded with 1900 tons of riprap. In this unfinished state the contemplated Plum Beach Lighthouse will now be forced to remain until congress in its beneficence sees fit to grant an extra appropriation of from $10,000 to $15,000, which, when placed at the disposition of the Lighthouse Board, will permit them either to construct the superstructure themselves, or place the work in the hands of a contractor. It is hoped that this congress will take action on the subject, as the establishment of a beacon at this point in the West Passage has already been long delayed.

APPENDIX E

Boring Log Excerpt taken for new bridge in general vicinity of Lighthouse showing findings roughly similar to what Ludlow found.

<table>
<tr><td colspan="2">BORING CONTRACTOR:
Warren George</td><td colspan="3">CE MAGUIRE, INC.
ARCHITECTS-ENGINEERS-PLANNERS
BORING LOG
TOWN, STATE: Jamestown, RI
PROJECT NAME: Jamestown Bridge
CEM NO. 12375.170 OFFICE: Providence</td><td colspan="3">SHEET 1 OF 3
LOCATION: Pier No.
HOLE NO: D 136
BORING TYPE: Casing w/mud
LINE & STA.: 57+27.60
OFFSET: 52.08L</td></tr>
</table>

BORING CONTRACTOR: Warren George	CE MAGUIRE, INC. ARCHITECTS-ENGINEERS-PLANNERS BORING LOG	SHEET 1 OF 3
LOG PREPARED BY: CONTR. ___ CEM _X_	TOWN, STATE: Jamestown, RI · PROJECT NAME: Jamestown Bridge · CEM NO. 12375.170 OFFICE: Providence	LOCATION: Pier No. · HOLE NO: D 136 · BORING TYPE: Casing w/mud · LINE & STA.: 57+27.60 · OFFSET: 52.08L

GROUND WATER OBSERVATIONS

AT ___ FT. AFTER ___ HOURS
AT ___ FT. AFTER ___ HOURS

	AUGER	CASING	SAMPLER	CORE BAR.
TYPE		SW	SS	NX
SIZE, I.D.		6"	1 3/8"	3" OD
HAMMER WT.		600#	140#	BIT.
HAMMER FALL		24"	30"	

SURFACE ELEV. -15.5
DATE STARTED-FINISHED: 11/3
BORING FOREMAN: T. Tirro
INSPECTOR: D. Stapleton
SOILS ENGR.: P. Aldinger

LOCATION OF BORING:

DEPTH BELOW MSL	CASING BLOWS PER FOOT	SAMPLE DEPTH FROM - TO	TYPE OF SAMPLE	BLOWS PER 6" ON SAMPLER 0-6	6-12	12-18	STRATA CHANGE DEPTH ELEV.	FIELD IDENTIFICATION OF SOIL & ROCK INCL. COLOR, LOSS OF WASH WATER, JOINTS IN ROCK, ETC.	NO.	PEN.	REC.
15.0							-15.5	Mudline			
								SILT, dark gray to black, clayey, trace sand and shell fragments, very soft, saturated	1		
20.0		19.0 to 21.5	D	Wt. of rock					1	18	12
25.0							-24.5	Casing settled to -24.5 under own weight			
	15										
	18										
	21										
	20										
30.0	38										
	38										
	38										
	38										
	50										
35.0	50						-34.5	Bottom of Casing			
		35.0 to 36.5	D	12	9	11		SAND, brown, silty, trace gravel, medium dense, saturated, subrounded	2	18	6
40.0											
		41.0 to 42.5	D	6	6	9		SAND, gray brown, silty trace gravel, medium dense, saturated, subrounded	3	18	12
45.0											
		46.0 to 47.5	D	10	11	12		SAND, gray brown, gravelly, trace silt, medium dense, saturated, subrounded	4	18	4
50.0											
		51.0 to 52.5	D	13	19	27		SAND, gray brown, silty trace gravel, dense saturated, subangular	5	18	9
55.0							-55.0				

Part of 1987 Boring Log for the <u>new</u> Jamestown Bridge. Shows borings into the Plum Beach Shoal from the same general vicinity as the lighthouse. Results appear to correspond roughly to findings of Engineer Ludlow's borings in 1896.

Courtesy of C.E. McGuire, Inc. and Rhode Island Department of Transportation.

APPENDIX F

Chronology of Construction of the Plum Beach Lighthouse
(Chapter III)

Information, obtained just before publication, from the 1896 Journal of the Lighthouse Board, indicates how remote the Light-House Board as a decision-making body actually was from the important issues facing the Third District Engineer. It appears that the Board's Engineer Secretary, John Millis, made all the important decisions, and that the Board, as if to fulfill legal requirements, caught up with formal actions long after the fact.

March 2, 1895	Appropriation of $20,000 makes possible site selection, survey and drawing of plans.
June 11, 1896	Appropriation of $40,000 "for finishing the establishment of a light and fog signal station at or near Plum Beach, Rhode Island." "The station is to be completed," the Board's report says, " before the close of navigation this winter."
July 9, 1896	Contract signed with I.H. Hathaway Company of Philadelphia for the erection of the lighthouse for $38,490.
July 13, 1896	Work begins in Providence on the construction of the wooden caisson at Hill's Wharf.
August 19, 1896	Wooden Caisson launched from wharf in Providence; building up of first two sections of cylinder done before floating the caisson down the bay.
September12, 1896	Third District Engineer Ludlow has finished a preliminary set of borings at and near the construction site; reports adverse findings to the Light-House Board; Caisson, recently towed from Providence is settled on the bottom of the bay over the construction site.

October 4, 1896	Board meets; rejects Hathaway's original bid of $42,000, as if contract for $38,490 had not already been signed in July and work begun. No discussion in minutes of Ludlow's Sept. 12 report.
October 23, 1896	Ludlow informs the contractor that the Board will at this time make no change in contract for the purpose ordering a deeper foundation. Work proceeds.
December 5&6, 1896	Cutting edge of caisson has reached 35' 3" below mean low water. Ludlow takes more borings from inside the caisson. Finds "quicksand" immediately below contract depth of 38 feet. Work stops.
December 7, 1896	Ludlow sends report with diagram to Board. Board meets same day. No mention in minutes of communication from Ludlow.
December 8, 1896	Board requests new proposal from Contractor.
December 9, 1896	Ludlow sends proposal by F.C. Arthur for Hathaway Company; Engineer Secretary of the Board, Millis, authorizes Ludlow to make new contract.
December 14, 1896	Engineer Secretary Millis writes the Secretary of the Treasury reporting Contractor's new proposal, stating that the Board has directed Ludlow "to enter into an agreement" with the contractor; and says "The Board" asks approval to enter into the agreement.
January 4, 1897	The Board meets; Engineer Committee recommends special appropriation of $9,000 to complete the lighthouse.
January 30, 1897	Caisson finished; contractor and workers leave; temporary beacon under charge of Captain Eaton initiated.
February, 1897	Installation of 1500 tons of rip rap begins.
June 1, 1897	Fog signal installed.

March 23, 1898	Third District Engineer Heap plans a temporary shelter on unfinished lighthouse so that Eaton can stay there when fog is coming. Says ". . . Station will never be a satisfactory aid to navigation until tower is built."
July 1, 1898	Appropriation of $9,000 for completing lighthouse.
September 12, 1898	Work begins.
January 16, 1899	After many delays caused by Tacony Iron, and by bad weather, in the face of more bad weather, contractor Toomey leaves without authority.
February 13, 1899	Revised contract with Toomey, & Co.
April, 1899	Work resumes.
June 1, 1899	Lighthouse is finished.

APPENDIX G

1911 Summary of Construction Costs

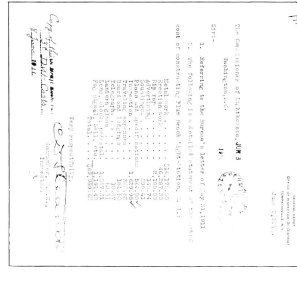

Summary of costs.
From National Archives.

Helme & Chandler Map, 1742.
From R.I. Historical Society Collection.

APPENDIX H

The Name, *Plum Beach*
(Chapter IV)

The first use we could discover of the name *Plum Beach* in reference to the area of shoreline beginning just north of the present Jamestown Bridge and going as far as Quarry Point to the south, is in a 1716 deed mentioned in J. R. Cole's *History of Washington and Kent Counties* on page 393. The deed in which Stephen Northrup and his wife Mary sell to Benjamin Northrup 150 acres includes the "Plum beach pond" as part of the boundary. The same family operated a ferry from North Ferry at Quarry Point to Jamestown between 1707 and 1815.

While it is true that the often copied Blaskowitz map made for the British government in 1777 shows "Plumb beach pt." in the vicinity of Duck Cove, in the approximate location of Wild Goose Point, and some other maps have apparently followed it, there is no reason to give more credence to the Blaskowitz map than to the Helme and Chandler map of 1742 which shows "Plumbbeach point" much closer to the location of the Plum Beach pond mentioned in the 1716 deed, and well known to the builders of the Plum Beach Light. Helme and Chandler shows this point as south of Rome's Point and Bissel's Cove, but leaves out Greene's Point. The fact is that both maps show discrepancies from the coastline as we know it today. Even allowing for shifting of beaches due to storm erosion, etc. their map-making accuracy has to be questioned.

We are indebted to Henry A. L. Brown, an experienced researcher in Rhode Island history for information from papers in his care written by John Brown Francis in the 1820's or 30's about what is probably the earliest recorded grounding on Plum Beach. A sloop, *Betsey,* owned by Benajah Williams was surreptitiously impounded by officers from the Customs House in Providence in December of 1808 or January of 1809. There was suspicion that Williams, Ephraim Bowen and others were attempting to violate the Embargo Act.

However, friends of the owner came stealthily by night to Providence, reequipped the impounded craft, and sailed it back to its home port in Pawtuxet. Shortly thereafter they took it down the bay and it went ashore at Plum Beach. Thereupon the ship was taken in by the Newport Customs House.

The name *Plum Point* became known only in the mid-1940's when developers having bought in 1942 the beautiful tract of woods and pastures on the hillside north of the Jamestown Bridge approach road (route 138), advertised the newly platted lots, which they put up for sale after World War II, as "Plum Point Shores." Gradually many people came to think of the point itself as "Plum Point" in a departure from over 200 years' tradition. Present day maps in referring to the Point itself seem to be divided between the earlier name "Plum Beach Point" and "Plum Point." In a way the bridge split up not only the tidal pond on the point but also people's sense of geography. The other aspect of division is that some people in both residential areas wanted to think of their area and their community as distinct from each other.

The name, *Barber's Heights*, came from a family that had a home near the present intersection of Boston Neck Road and Fleetwood Drive. However Freeman Tefft in a bid for fanciness changed the spelling when he named "Barbour's Heights Cottage."

APPENDIX I

Excerpts from Unpublished Narrative by Nathan M. Wright, Jr. of the 1938 Hurricane as observed from the offices of his Mortgage Guarantee & Title Company at 85 Westminster St.
(Chapter V)

The morning of September 21, 1938 was unseasonably warm. By noon-time the weather was sultry, like a summer's day. . . .

On an inspection trip to the upper floors of the building, I had occasion to look at the roof of the building next west, and I noticed that the tin roof indicated that it might be torn off. In fact, it was bellowing so hard at the time that I suggested to tenants whose offices were on the fourth floor that it might be prudent to keep back from the windows. . . . Sheets of driven rain were sweeping around the southeast corner of the Industrial Trust Building, running parallel to the roof and driven with such force that it looked more like snow than water. . . About four o'clock it was difficult for pedestrians to navigate on Westminster Street . . . At five o'clock the wind was blowing harder than any of us had ever seen it blow before. . .

. . .I attempted to put through another call to my home, but was unable to make any further out-going calls from our office switch board. While standing in the outer office talking to Doris Mathewson, our switch board operator, there was a tremendous crash at the window in back of Doris. My first reaction was that, in addition to the tremendous storm, we were having a thunder storm. It developed that one of the six chimneys on the building next west, had been blown down and crashed against our window on the second floor, scattering glass across the room. . . Broken brick was piled on the out side of the window ledge as proof of what happened.

Right after the crash we were surprised to see water filling the streets. . . .

About 5:15 o'clock the lights dimmed momentarily and then went out. The current was not turned on again for some ten or eleven days.

In the meantime we realized that we were in the middle of a hurricane. The air was filled with all sorts of flying objects, consisting of glass, gutters, and conductors, and in our immediate vicinity innumerable awnings with their three-sided heavy metal frames. A few minutes later most of the show windows on Westminster Street, from the Arcade down to the Turks Head Building, were blown into the street almost simultaneously. The glass filled the air like flakes of snow and was driven with terrific force towards Tribune Square. Such pedestrians as happened to be around the Turks Head Building protected themselves as best they could by stepping into doorways. . .

The water continued to rise at a rapid rate and as far as we could see upn and down Westminster Street and across Exchange Place on the north everything was under water. The wind increased in intensity. The clock at the Arcade had long since been torn from its moornings and was hanging by a single wire and in itself was a menacing pendulum.. . .Tin roofs were being rolled up by the gale and blown across the street and on neighboring buildings. The tin roof on the building next west of us was rolled up in many places and was carried almost to Exchange Place. . . .

On the north side of the building we witnessed several rescues. In one case a young woman was rescued by a human chain from the southwest corner of the Fearney property. She was standing in water well over her waist, apparently dazed and uncertain what to do. In the meantime portions of the tin roof on the building next west were blowing off. Some young men finally worked their way down to the stranded girl, and led her to Exchange Place and across to the Industrial Trust Building.

About 6:15 the water was up to the tops of automobiles stationed in the streets and was still rising. The wind was blowing harder and harder. It seemed that the windows on the south and the southwest would be blown in at any time. The water on the street was so rough that the street was a sea of white-caps. . . .

. . .The storm increased in intensity as time went on. . . .We saw a white enameled refrigerator floating in Exchane Place. . . .Some automobiles were carried along by the current . . . Bridge timbers floated through the streets.

It was an awesome sight to look out into the streets of the city and see them so deep in water that no one could get out of the buildings. People were frightened.

Approximately at 7:10 the water ceased rising.

Automobile horns commenced to blow, electric lights on the automobiles began to burn, signal burglar and traffic alarms began to ring and the town was bedlam let loose. Short circuits of electric wire systems had started in their work.

The wind subsided at approximately 7:20 and in a few minutes we were able to detect the waters receding. . . .

Shortly before the turn of the tide we observed a man stripped to the waist hanging on to the barber sign on the building where Schmidt's Cutlery Store is located on the south side of Westminster Streets. A few minutes later the man had disappeared from sight. His body was found about nine o'clock that night in front of the Phenix building where Blanding's Store is located. His body was found under the wheels of a truck. . . .

Any one who did not go through the night in downtown Providence never realized what a fearful sight it was to see the water rising with no way of telling to what height it might eventually reach.

APPENDIX J

Partial List of Keepers of the Plum Beach Light

Information is available from the Register of Keepers at the National Archives including from 1845 to 1812. Later records are at the Personnel Records Center in St. Louis, which does not allow divulgence of information without permission from the individual or a death certificate!

From the Register:

Joseph L. Eaton,	Formally appointed June 5, 1897 after serving since February, through June,1899
Judson G. Allen	July 1, 1899
George Ehrhardt	March 19, 1904
George Tray,	March 20, 1911

From the recollections of informants for this book:

Charles Ormsby	From around 1915 to mid-1920's
Captain Robarge	1920's ?
"Moon" Mullins	1920's ?
Edwin S. Babcock	Substitute Keeper from early 1920's to 1938
Reuben Phillips	Keeper from late twenties or early thirties until retirement 1938 or 1939
John Otto Ganze	Assistant Keeper, 1933 or 34 until retirement of R. Phillips, then Ganze would have been Keeper briefly until going to Spectacle Island in early 1940
Two Coast Guard men	names unknown, reportedly alternated in serving this light until it was closed in 1941

BIBLIOGRAPHY AND SOURCES

General

With the exception of published books and a few of the many newspaper references, copies of all the documents used in preparing this book have been donated to The Special Collections Department of the University Library at the University of Rhode Island, at Kingston, Rhode Island.

Major sources of information about lighthouses in the United States used in this book are as follows:

The National Archives, Washington D C 20408. For the purpose of lighthouse research the most important part of the Archives is the Judicial, Fiscal, and Social Branch, Civil Archives Division. This branch has an extensive collection of original documents which are available for the public to examine by appointment at the Archives and copies of which are available by mail upon sending specific requests and fees. Given the large volume of requests coming into this branch, the copying and mailing process is time-consuming. The branch has a general information sheet "Records Relating to Lighthouses" which summarizes the different types of lighthouse material they have.

The types of material from the Judicial, Fiscal, and Social Branch on the Plum Beach Light used in the preparation of this book are over one hundred pages of letters from bound volumes which I selected on the basis of index slips titled "Plum Beach, R. I. Light Station" (not to be confused with Plum Beach, New York, or Plum Island, Maine), clipping file material, including excerpts from the *Annual Reports* of the Light-House Board regarding the Board's recommendations to Congress about expenditures for the construction and maintenance of the light, contracts, engineering reports, information for Plum Beach from the *Registers of Keepers*, 1845-1912, and information relating to Plum Beach from the Journals of the Light-House Board, 1852-1908.

The National Archives Military Reference Branch of the Military Archives Division has information about some of the District Engineers from the U. S. Army Corps of Engineers. The Still Pictures Branch has pictures of Plum Beach and other Lighthouses; The Cartographic and Architectural Branch has plans and drawings of some lighthouses but not the Plum Beach. The General Branch has logbooks for some lighthouses, but not for Plum Beach or Whale Rock. I have made extensive search for the logs of both stations, but these potentially rich sources of historical data appear to have been lost forever.

The Office of the United States Coast Guard Historian at U.S. Coast Guard Headquarters, 2100 2nd St, S.W. Washington, D. C., 20593-301, has the insightful knowledgeable resource of the Historian, Robert L. Scheina, Ph.D. and a small library including files on individual lighthouses and Annual Lists of Aids to Navigation containing technical and identifying data for every aid (floating or lighthouse) in the United States.

The Library of the United States Coast Guard Academy at New London, Connecticut, includes an extensive collection of books on United States and foreign lighthouses, the Annual Reports of the Light House Board, U. S. Lighthouse Service Bulletins, Annual Lists of Aids to Navigation and an extensive collection on microfilm of original engineers' drawings and plans for U. S. Lighthouses, including many pages of Plum Beach.

The originals of the microfilmed Plum Beach plans and plans of other lighthouses at the Academy are to be found along with other Plum Beach plans (not at the Academy) at the Coast Guard Shore Facilities Design and Construction Section SMD New York, Building 107, Governor's Island, New York 10004.

Sources of Information in Rhode Island about Rhode Island Lighthouses are:

The Exhibit and Brochure, "Rhode Island's Lighthouses" prepared by Sarah Gleason for the Department of Environmental Management, and the Rhode Island Historical Preservation Commission to be permanently housed at the Museum established by the Rhode Island Parks Association at Beavertail.

Specific entries in the Rhode Island File Card Catalogue at the Providence Public Library.

The State Archives at the State House, Providence, R. I. while it has nothing on the Plum Beach Light, has some interesting lighthouse documents going back to the eighteenth century.

United States Government Documents at the Rockefeller Library of Brown University and at the University of Rhode Island Library.

PERIODICALS:

The Providence [Daily] Journal and *The Providence Sunday Journal,* dates for the purpose of the Plum Beach Light 1880-1984 found on microfilm at the Rockefeller Library at Brown University, The Providence Public Library, and the University of Rhode Island Library. The *Evening Bulletin* at the Providence Public Library, and The U. R. I. Library.

Newport History, Bulletin of the Newport Historical Society. Spring, 1971 Number 142 Vol.44 part 2 Series on Rhode Island Lighthouses including Plum Beach and Whale Rock, by Richard Champlin. See acknowledgment comment in Introduction of this book.

The Wickford *Standard*, dates inclusive for this study: 1895-1941 and its successor, The *Standard-Times*,1983-1985. The *Standard* filled a lot of its pages with National syndicated news summaries and features. Aside from writers from different villages in the area who sent in weekly notes mainly covering social events and the coming and going of people, the *Standard* apparently made no use of reporters or reporting techniques to pursue stories. The most important North Kingstown news came mostly in short news items of one or two sentences at the most, derived from the editor's personal contacts and information brought in by townspeople. As a result there is no expansive treatment of most local news items. However, taken in aggregate, the many short items help to provide a broad picture of what it was like to live in North Kingstown during those years. The lengthy 1899 articles on the Sea View Rail Road are an exception to the short-item pattern. The *Standard-Times* assumes people get national and international news elsewhere, and provides in-depth coverage of local stories and issues.

The *Standard* and the *Standard-Times* are found on microfilm at the North Kingstown Free Library.

Providence Journal of Commerce later known as *Providence Board of Trade Journal* for the purposes of this study, dates 1892-1901, Copies at R.I. Historical Society Library, Rockefeller and Providence Public Library. Great emphasis on maritime commerce and manufacturing.

BOOKS:

Ancient and Modern Light-Houses by Major D. P. Heap, Corps of Engineers, United States Army, Ticknor And Company, Boston, 1889. Written after Heap has served four years as Engineer Secretary of the Light-House Board, and as Engineer Officer in various districts; blow-by-blow description of the planning and construction of the Rothersand Light and the Fourteen Foot Bank Light, prototypes of the pneumatic caisson type of construction used at Plum Beach. Thorough covering of national lighthouse administration in Europe and U. S. Includes muted criticism of congresssional funding of the Board. The Providence Athenaeum has this book.

America's Lighthouses by Francis Ross Holland, Greene, 1972.

Rhode Island, A History, by William G. Mcloughlin; part of the States and Nation series administered by the American Association for State and Local History; published by W. C. Norton and Company, New York, 1978, 1986.

A *Productive Monopoly, The Effect of Railroad Control on New England Coastal Steamship Lines, 1870—1916*, by William Leonhard Taylor, Brown University Press, Providence, 1970. A study of the transportation system and its relationship to the economy of the area. The appendices include tables with a lot of data on the steamship lines.

Chapter I

Captain Eaton:

Personal conversations with Mr. and Mrs. Robert Eaton, of Narragansett, Rhode Island. Mr. Eaton is a grandson of the Captain. They have a wealth of pictures, clippings and notes about Captain Eaton and his ancestors at South Ferry. Their memorabilia include the Bible from the *Rhode Island*. Mrs. Eaton has typed up the anonymous contemporary account of South Ferry and the Eatons from unidentified newspaper clippings, and a copy is on file at the Willett Free Library in Saunderstown.

Saunderstown and Stillman Saunders:

Saunderstown by Irving C. Sheldon with Drawings by Shirley W. Sheldon, 1985. This book is based on documentary research, the author's interviews with people involved, and his direct personal knowledge of the history he tells.

Maritime History:

State of Rhode Island and Providence Plantations at the End of the Century: A History, edited by Edward Field, Volume Two, The Mason Publishing Company, Boston, 1902; Chapter IV, "The Sea Trade and its Development." By Robert Grieve.

A *Productive Monopoly*; see in General section above.

Providence Journal of Commerce, see in General section.

Identifying features of lighthouses:

See in the Light-House Board's Annual Lists of Aids to Navigation.

Chapter II

<u>The Light-House Board,The Bureau of Lighthouses and the Lighthouse Service</u>:

Light-Houses Ancient and Modern, see in General section above, especially Chapter XVII.

America's Lighthouses, see in General section, above.

Chronology of Aids to Navigation and The Old Lighthouse Service, 1716-1939 pamphlet by Truman R. Strobridge, U.S. Coast Guard Historian, U. S. Coast Guard Historical Chronology Program, 1974, Office of Coast Guard Historian, see in General section above.

Sentinel of the Coasts, The Log of a Lighthouse Engineer by George R. Putnam, Commissioner of Lighthouses, retired, W. W. Norton, New York, 1937, pages 118-127 and 154-159. With the reorganization of 1910 Putnam became the first Commissioner of Lighthouses and served for twenty-five years. Within five years after his retirement lighthouses went under the jurisdiction of the Coast Guard. He advocates the ideas of decentralization and simplicity of administration which were part of the reorganization of 1910.

<u>General U. S. History</u>:

Political and Social History of the United States 1829-1925 by Arthur M. Schlesinger, Macmillan, New York, 1929.

<u>Frank M. Burrough and the Burrough Family</u>:

Nine letters and cards from Frank M. Burrough to Senator Aldrich are found in The Papers of Nelson W. Aldrich, see below. The 1882 and 1884 letters of Burrough to Aldrich about Plum Beach are also found in the Plum Beach Light Station correspondence at the National Archives, see above in General Section. The 1882 Plum Beach Letter is not in the Aldrich Papers; the 1884 letter in the Archives is a secretary's copy, the original of which is in the Aldrich Papers.

Correspondence from Burrough to the Lighthouse Board is quoted, reported, and/or evaluated by the *Providence Journal of Commerce* issues of January, 1896, June 1896, April, 1898, and June 1898.

Frank Burrough, his father James, his great uncle, Robert Sterry Burrough, Sr. and the family business activities are mentioned in the article on Frank's cousin, Robert S. Burrough, on pages 474-474 of the *Biographical Cyclopedia* at the Rhode Island Historical Society.

The Providence Directory and The Providence City Directory annual issues, for this study, from 1827-1903 including residences of Burrough family members.

The Providence Daily Journal of May 27, 1903, Obituary of Frank M. Burrough.

The author would welcome hearing of any additional information about Frank M. Burrough.

Nelson W. Aldrich:

The Papers of Nelson W. Aldrich: in the Manuscript Division of the Library of Congress; the papers were presented in three installments by the family and one installment by the Seminary of Our Lady Of Providence, of the Diocese of Providence.

In addition to the correspondence from Burrough mentioned above this collection includes correspondence from various officers of the Providence and Stonington Steamship Company referred to in Chapter II of this book, and from others about maritime issues.

There is a complete index of the Aldrich Papers in the Reference Department of the Rockefeller Library of the Brown University Library. The papers are available on microfilm series.

Nelson W. Aldrich: The Making of the "General Manager of the United States," 1841-1886, by Jerome L. Sternstein, Ph.D., an unpublished doctoral dissertation for the Department of History, Brown University, June, 1968; available at the Rockefeller Library. Mr. Sternstein, now Professor of History at Brooklyn College, is preparing for publication a full length biography of Aldrich.

Rhode Island, A History, see in general section above.

"Dynasty," an article by Nelson W. Aldrich, Jr. in the *Sunday Journal Magazine* of June 26, 1988, an adaptation by Doug Cumming from Aldrich's new book, *Old Money*, published by Alfred A. Knopf, Inc. presents some conclusions about Senator Aldrich similar to those in this book. However the book *Old Money* was published too close to the printing of this book to be considered by the author. It is clear, however, that the author of *Old Money* makes a departure from the efforts of earlier descendants of the Senator to whitewash the character of this many-sided influential person.

Lighthouse design and history:

The Evolution of the Lighthouse Tower by Dr. Robert L. Scheina is a pamphlet at the Coast Guard Historian's Office, see above in

General section. This article and Dr. Scheina's discussions with the author have provided important technological and historical perspective for this chapter.

Ancient and Modern Light-Houses, see above.

Chronology, see above.

The Providence and Stonington Steamship Company:

A Productive Monopoly, see in General section above. The P. and S. along with other New England lines is discussed in chapters and appendices throughout the book.

At the End of the Century by Field see in Chapter I, above.

"Sound Steamers" on page 16 of the October 4, 1896 *Sunday Journal*, a full page history, with illustrations, of the P. and S. and earlier lines on the occasion of the end of the P. and S. as a separate company.

Letters in The Aldrich Papers, see above.

"The Nicaragua Canal Board, 1893-1896" Chapter VII of *William Ludlow, Engineer, Governor, Soldier* see below under Chapter III.

Providence Daily Journal articles of April 12, May 2, and May 5, 1896 on the Ludlow report.

The Path Between the Seas—The Creator's of the Panama canal 1870–1914 by David McCullough, Simon & Schuster, New York, 1977. Pages 182-241.

Chapter III

Newspaper reports on construction of the Plum Beach Light:

The Providence Journal: August 18, August 19, August 20, 1896 on the floating of the caisson at Providence, includes the direct quote from F. C. Arthur; February 8, 1897 summarizes the method of construction, explains the difficulty with establishing caisson depth, and the interruption of construction; February 15, 1819 about legislation proposed in Congress to deal with damage and protect from future damage, after 1918 freeze.

The Wickford *Standard* : Many brief articles beginning October 9, 1896, and ending May 26, 1899. The final reference is the *Standard's* version of the Notice to Mariners. Presumbably the Notice also appears in the *Journal*, but we have not found it.

Construction Technology and the Construction of The Plum Beach Light:

Consultation with Dr. Robert L. Scheina, Coast Guard Historian, and with Professor Armand Silva, of the Department of Oceanic Engineering, University of Rhode Island.

Ancient and Modern Lighthouses by Major Heap, see in General section above, Chapters XI and XII.

February 8, 1896 *Journal* article, above.

Plum Beach Light Station letters, contract, and reports in the National Archives from January, 1896 through September, 1899, June 5, 1911, February, 1918 through June, 1924. Especially those to and from H. M. Adams, William Ludlow, D. P. Heap, F. C. Arthur, Hathaway, and Co., H. Toomey, and Company.

The caisson technology in the Brooklyn Bridge: *The Great Bridge* by David McCullough, Simon and Schuster, New York, 1972. There is also a book, title and author unknown to this author about the bridge built by Eads over the Mississippi at St. Louis, which was ther first use of the pneumatic caisson technology for a bridge in this country.

Information on the November, 1898, *Portland* gale from *Shipwrecks Around the New England* by William P. Quinn, Lower Cape Publishing Co., Orleans, Massachusetts, 1979.

Biographical Information on the Engineers:

Cullum's Register of West Point graduates published by the West Point Alumni Association, several editions during the last decades of the nineteenth century. The graduates are listed by class and by class standing; to follow the continuing careers of individual graduates look for updated entries in succeeding editions. Books at Rockefeller Library.

William Ludlow, Engineer, Governor, Soldier. by Eugene Vincent McAndrews, Ph.D., doctoral dissertation for the Department of History, Kansas State University, Manhattan Kansas, 1973. On microfilm from Xerox University Microfilms, Ann Arbor, Michigan 46106. The papers from the prepartion of this book at the University of Rhode Island Library Special Collections Department, include the entire McAndrews dissertation copied on the microfilm machine. The dissertation is part of the Military Affairs doctoral program at the University of Kansas and has been used here with much appreciated cooperation and permission of Professor Robin Higham. Unfortunately Mr. McAndrews eventually died from illnesses suffered while writing this book which rescues from obscurity the career of a remarkable person.

Chapter IV

<u>The Sea View Rail Road</u>:

Through the Woods and Across the Fields to Narragansett Pier by G. Edward Prentice, 1983.

Brief unpublished manuscript by Edwin S. Babcock copied from original held by Helen Dwelly.

The Providence Daily Journal, June 17, 1899, and *Sunday Journal* article of June 18, 1899 about the inaugural run from Wickford to Narragansett Pier.

The Wickford *Standard*, articles from April 14, 1899 to August 11, 1899, especially the June 23, 1899 article on the inaugural run.

<u>Plum Beach, Barber's Heights</u>:

Personal experience of the author over the course of 54 years, Conversations with Leicester Bradner and other Plum Beach people during this era about the earlier days.

Interviews for this book, 1984-1988, with John Bradner, Bill Dwelly, Helen Dwelly, Florence Foskett, Irving Hazard.

Letter to the author from Nancy Farin, March 26, 1984.

UNPUBLISHED ARTICLES:

"A Trip to the Lighthouse" by Leicester Bradner, around 1917.

"Plum Beach" a history by Alice Richardson Davis revised by Priscilla Teeden, in Plum Beach Club Archives.

"Some Memories and Some History of Plum Beach, North Kingstown, R. I." by John Bradner, on file at Reference Department, North Kingstown Free Library.

NEWSPAPER ARTICLE:

"So long, Babbie's—new change for old corner" by Linda Watts Jackim, in *The Standard-Times* December 12, 1985, an article to which Mr. and Mrs. Dwelly, Betty Kulasewski, Diane Kulasewski, William Gadrow, Robert Hazard, and the author of this book contributed; written at the time the Babbie's tradition in the businesses at the corner of Plum Beach Road and Boston Neck Road came to an end.

BOOK:

History of Washington and Kent Counties, by J. R. Cole, 1889, pages 372 and 393, reference to Plum Beach Pond in 1716 deed.

Chapter V

The 1917-1918 Freeze:

Interviews with John Bradner, Earl Caswell, Irving Hazard.

PUBLISHED REPORTS:

The Barber's Heights *Clamshell,* 1918 Winter issue, No. 4, January Number

"That Winter of 1917" by Oliver H. Stedman appearing in *The Spectator*, February 8, 1977 and March 6, 1979, courtesy of Irving Sheldon.

The Wickford *Standard* articles January 4, 1918, January 11, 1918, January 18, 1918, and March 29, 1918.

Richard Champlin's articles on Plum Beach and Whale Rock in *Newport History*, see in General Section, above

The September 21,1938, Hurricane:

BOOKS:

A Wind to Shake the World, The Story of the 1938 Hurricane, by Everett S. Allen, Little Brown and Company, Boston, 1976.

The Great Hurricane and Tidal Wave-Rhode Island, September 21, 1938, designed and produced by the Artgravure Department of *The Providence Journal*, published by The Providence Journal Company, 1938. A comprehensive discussion of many aspects of the storm and its effect with excellent pictures, a classic.

Kindly Lights, forthcoming book by Sarah Gleason.

NEWSPAPERS, ETC:

The Providence Journal, September 21, 1938-September 24, 1938, and December 8, 1939.

The Wickford *Standard*, September 23 and September 30, 1938.

The Rhode Island Pendulum of East Greenwich, September 15, September 22, and September 29, 1938.

"Lighting the Way" by Sarah C. Gleason in *Save the Bay*, June/July, 1886, about John Ganze in the Plum Beach Light and the Sakonnet Light.

"September 21, 1938" by Richmond Crolius in the *Delta Phi Record*, December, 1938.

Champlin articles in *Newport History*, see above. "Whale Rock" article presents testimony and interpretations about the destruction of that lighthouse.

UNPUBLISHED WRITINGS:

A ten-page article by Nathan M. Wright, Jr., the storm from the vantage point of 85 Westminster St. Courtesy of the Wright family.

Diary of Cynthia Gowdy (Mrs. Mahlon) 1936-1940
Log of the *Hammonton* at U.R.I. Special Collections

INTERVIEWS:

John O. Ganze, 3 occasions in 1984

Helen Dwelly and Bill Dwelly, on many occasions 1984-1988

Alda Kaye, 2 occasions 1987 and 1988

Peter C. Crolius, 1984

Richmond Crolius, telephone interview, 1984

Charles Cook, February, 1984, and June, 1988

Charles Arnold, June 1988

Mahlon Wright and Jacqueline Wright, June, 1988

Doug Arnold, 2 occasions June 1988

Chapter VI

The Repair and Closing of the Plum Beach Light:

Governmental communications about repairs following the Hurricane and closing of the lighthouse come from The General Correspondence File 1911-1939 of the Bureau of Lighthouses.

Clippings in Scrapbook Collection of Mahlon G. Wright, see below.

Interview with John Ganze, see in Chapter V.

The opening of the Jamestown Bridge and closing of the Saunderstown ferry:

Providence Journal and *Sunday Journal* articles July 25, 1940 through August 4, 1940.

Wickford *Standard* articles July 19, 1940 through August 9, 1940.

Clippings in Scrapbook, see below. Especially July 25 *Journal* article, July 27 *Evening Bulletin* article, and July 27 *Newport Daily News*.

Interviews, Waldo M. Wright, June, 1988.

The construction of the Bridge:

Clipping scrapbook of articles collected by Mahlon G. Wright from a variety of newspapers during 1939-1940; Mr. Wright is donating this book to the University of Rhode Island Library Special Collections Department.

The Opposition to the Bridge:

New York Times July 7, 1940 article

Conversation with Nathan M. Wright, Jr. 1972

Interview with Irving Hazard, 1985

Interviews with Helen Murray, Mahlon G. Wright, Jacqueline Wright, Robert Bradner, William Bradner, Helen Reid, Richard Reid, June, 1988.

The Keepers after the Closing:

"So long, Babbie's" article in Wickford *Standard*, see in Chapter IV, above.

Interviews cited in Chapter V above with John Ganze, Bill and Helen Dwelly, and Alda Kaye.

Lighthouse Structure after Closing:

Consultation with Kenneth Morse, 1988

Coast Guard documents cited in text

Newspaper articles cited in text

University of Rhode Island internal communications

Telephone conversations with Terry Cramer, 1985 and 1989 National Archives documents 1895, 1933, 1953-67; letter to the author from Commander R. A. Brunelle, District Legal Officer of the First Coast Guard District, March 8, 1989 with copies of Light-House Board correspondence of 1893-1895.